To Duane,
You have made such a huge
difference in my life, my friend!
Keep on reaching and teaching, and
Keep on...

LOVIN' LIFE

A Guide to Authentic Self-Discovery

Garvin DeShazer

Love,

Gar

i

LOVIN'LIFE

A Guide to Authentic Self-Discovery

Text and graphics copyright © 2016 by Garvin DeShazer, All rights reserved.

No part of this publication may be reproduced in any form or by any means, including scanning, photocopying, or otherwise without prior written permission of the author.

To Cynthia

Have I told you lately ...?

To Courtney and Angela

Always remember ...

ACKNOWLEDGEMENTS

This book, perhaps more than many others, is the product of deep introspection. It has emerged from a lifetime of passionately pursuing truth and understanding, moving first in one direction, then another, eventually discovering that, in the broadest sense, most paths generally circle back to connect with each other. These pages reflect the influences of various teachers who have shared their wisdom in many ways. Whether our sojourns have merely met for a moment or lasted a lifetime, I am profoundly grateful for each one.

In particular, I want to thank my family—my parents, long since passed, who each loved me the best they were able; my brothers, Maurice, George and Chuck, their wives and their children, every one of them an extraordinary teacher and example in his or her own way; my wife, Cynthia, who taught me the meaning of unconditional love before I ever heard the term, whose unwavering love was the only light I was able to see in my darkest days, and who quietly and powerfully sustained me with her love even when I was incapable of receiving it; Cynthia's parents, Phyllis (no longer with us, though her memory lives on) and Bernie (my hero, a truly wise and gentle man) who filled her to overflowing with their amazing love in the first place; and my daughters, Courtney and Angela, the most precious and abiding gifts any father could ever have.

I've come to see that gratitude is never an obligation, but always a privilege, and in that spirit, I wish to thank Ken Peterson for turning the key; Duane Smotherman, Lou Dozier, Barbara Fagan and David Gilcrease for teaching me the difference between victimhood and the true empowerment of accountability; Rich and Yvonne Dutra-St. John, and all the team at Challenge Day, for challenging me to see the world in a different way; Galaxy, for showing me what living always in service looks like; Dr. Tom Reed for sharing with me his vision for a naturally energized planet, along with Bill Orr, David Orr, Kathie Nafie, Nolan and Das, for working untiringly toward the fulfillment of that vision; Mike Sheffield and the team at The Sheffield Group, for giving me a sustainable platform from which to pursue my dreams; Dr. Karen Paschal, Dr. Michelle Medrano and Rev. Kathryn McDowell for providing invaluable spiritual guidance; and Dr. Greg Bear, Donna Baer, Andy and Lori Carrillo and the entire Real Love community for bringing it all together in one clear focus, that the meaning of life has, as its center point, the choice to give, receive and *be* love.

Beyond the specifics, I have been blessed with several friends who have been so much a part of my life, for so long, that they have a continuing influence in all that I do. These include Dennis Riley, Bill Mayer, Brenda Sampson, Mike Sheffield, Nolan Hale, Nicki Keohohou, Ken Lind and Barbi Snow.

For direct assistance with this book, I wish to express my sincere appreciation and gratitude to my publishing and marketing coach, Monte Taylor; to my writing advisor and wordsmith extraordinaire, Jon Ward; to my psychology resource and frequent sounding board, Kelli Pacicco, to the final authority for all things grammatical, George DeShazer; and, of course, to Cynthia, who has listened patiently to every sentence, and every revision, so many times—thank you!

Finally, my expressions of gratitude would be incomplete without an acknowledgement of the role played by a dozen or so ruby-throated hummingbirds, seen dancing in a dizzying frenzy of joy one afternoon, just off the side of Shaw Butte ... message received!

Table of Contents

INTRODUCTION

What if you awoke one morning to find that you had been magically transported to an alternate universe, to a world where *everything* was different from anything you had ever experienced? Every sight, every sound, every sensation, the air you breathe, even gravity—all different. With no familiar points of reference, how could you possibly make sense of it all? And yet, if you were certain your very survival depended upon rapidly learning the rules of your new environment, wouldn't you give that effort your all?

Each of us has already had such an experience. It's called birth.

From the moment you arrived on earth, you have been asking questions, some out loud but most unconsciously, attempting to understand the rules of the game of life. Every time you've framed a subconscious question, you've sought, in one way or another, to find the true answer or, at least, an answer that's functional for the moment.

Could this distinction—between the answer that's true and the one that's merely functional in the moment—be far more important than most of us have ever actually taken time to consider? Could it be that, in our urgency to establish a functional framework in which to survive, we may have missed something vital to the essence of our living?

We all came to this life pre-programmed with a need to quickly find a set of answers we could live with, to define our basic paradigm and then commit to the rightness of it. That's just a basic efficiency, isn't it? After all, with everything each of us has going on in our lives at any given moment, we simply don't have time to constantly revisit every prior decision about our most fundamental beliefs, do we?

But if, having settled upon a paradigm that *seems* to work, meeting at least the test of survival, we conclude that we have life all figured out and begin to close our minds to new ideas; ceasing, in the interest of efficiency and comfort, to consider alternate perspectives and possibilities, don't we necessarily relegate ourselves to lives of mediocrity, at best? No matter how unintentional, don't the consequences of allowing ourselves to rest in our rightness always seem to confirm the constraints we've unwittingly imposed upon our lives and our happiness with our self-limiting beliefs?

Our core set of definitions about who we are, why we're here, what we value, how we relate to others, what is the nature of reality—our basic operating system—is comprised of a worldview, but more particularly a self-view. Each of us has a need to understand not just how the world works, but how we fit into it.

Like a computer, our operating system runs mainly in the background. Yet, this system of beliefs, this "paradigm of reality" controls every aspect of our lives. It is the lens through which our minds—both conscious and subconscious—see, and interpret (assign meaning to) every piece of input we receive.

Given the important role this "operating system" plays in our lives, might we find it useful to consider "updating the system" periodically, by challenging our paradigms, beginning with the foundational elements?

No promise of comfort is to be inferred as to the undertaking of such an endeavor. This is work made noble by both the courage required in the process and the transformative results that will surely follow in every aspect of your life. The magnitude of those results will be determined entirely by the commitment and passion with which you choose to embrace this quest.

So what is the purpose of this book? It is intended to serve as a roadmap, to help you discover the truth about you. As ambitious as it may sound, this book is offered as a tool you can use to facilitate your self-guided tour of life, the universe, God and everything. While this may seem to be a daunting task, my hope is that you will find it both achievable and disproportionately rewarding.

The following pages are filled with big questions. They are written in first person, but not my first person. Instead they are in *your* first person, meaning they are to be read in your own voice. My hope is that your reading of this book will be a profoundly personal and joy-filled exploration of who you are and who you can become, a dialogue with your deepest inner Self, that part of you that lives at the point where we are all connected.

Namaste,
Garvin DeShazer

Chapter 1

TRUTH

Who am I?

What Am I?

Don't I really need to explore the second question before I can fully answer the first?

What Does It Mean To Be Human?

Am I the current result of an endless series of accidents and naturally selective dead ends, beginning with a spontaneous origination of life on a previously dead lump of rock in a nondescript corner of the universe? Or, am I the deliberate creation of the one, true God, formed in His image as an eternal, individual soul; a potential heir to heaven's treasures or a denizen of the deep in the making, placed here to test my faith?

Are these the only possibilities?

Could there be a scenario in which I am neither consigned to the meaninglessness of random chance nor asked to reject the preponderance of evidence before me in favor of blind faith and willful ignorance?

Is that self-aware essence I think of as my "mind" the inevitable, bio-electro-chemical product of physical evolution? Or, is the physical reality I accept as oh-so-real actually a manifestation of a far larger mind, an all-encompassing "I Am" that exists in a realm beyond the limits of matter, energy, space and time?

How can I begin to answer such questions?

How have I come to my current framework of understanding? For the most part, haven't I just accepted someone else's beliefs, adopting them as my own? Whether from parents, siblings, teachers or other individuals of influence in my life, hasn't most of what I hold as true been handed down to me with little critical examination? Doesn't that leave me, if I dare to consider it, with a very important question?

13

Are the things I've been told, and that I have adopted as my most fundamental beliefs, based in truth or lies?

It does seem reasonable to accept the premise that the people closest to me intended to be truthful, doesn't it? After all, I don't generally start the day saying, "I *could* be loving and truthful today with the people I care about, particularly the children who are most vulnerable and susceptible to being misled, but instead, I think I'll just screw up their lives," do I? With some sociopathic exceptions, don't most people sincerely attempt to give sound guidance to the children in their lives? Isn't it likely that this was also the case for my parents?

But is that the real question? Were the good intentions of my parents and teachers sufficient to guarantee the accuracy of the content they provided me? If they were less than rigorous in obtaining the information they passed on to me, or if they were unknowingly misinformed by those who taught them, where does that leave me?

At what point must I accept responsibility for my own understanding?

Before I go further down this path, shouldn't I pause to determine whether what I've been taught really is suspect? After all, isn't it possible that everything I was raised to believe is, actually, the absolute truth?

But if so, what am I to make of the countless other "absolute truths" held, and vigorously defended, by the billions of co-habitants with whom I share this planet? Aren't their "absolute truths" often mutually exclusive with mine? If I'm right, don't they necessarily have to be wrong?

And, of course, they see this question the same way, don't they, only with their being right and me being wrong?

Isn't this how we've always derived our views about "us" and "them"? Isn't this how we have justified prejudice, discrimination, war and genocide?

If we could all set aside our individual egos for just a moment, doesn't it seem more likely that we are all wrong, to some degree? That none of us has achieved perfection? That we are all seekers of truth, some of whom may have glimpsed its edges, but every one of us is still a work in progress?

But that's not so easy to do, is it?

I defend most fiercely those lessons I've learned from personal experience, don't I, particularly when I've had the same experience many times, or when that experience has been seasoned with pain? But if these lessons subsequently prove to be wrong, the fact that I've affirmed and reaffirmed them in my own voice makes them the hardest lies to let go, doesn't it?

If I close my eyes and imagine for just a moment that I am two years old again, playing in the front yard on a spring day, can if feel the sun shining warm on my back as I squat down to pick a bright yellow dandelion? Can I detect the slight hint of a breeze as it wafts the sweet smell of fresh-mowed grass from my neighbor's yard? As a movement catches my eye and a beautiful monarch butterfly lifts itself on magnificent wings and flits just above my reach, am I transfixed with a sense of wonder? Do I run, in rapturous awe, with arms extended, laughing, jumping, and living entirely in that moment?

But when a powerful arm suddenly yanks me into the air, and a big hand comes down hard on my backside, as an angry voice shouts in my ear, "DON'T RUN OUT IN THE STREET, YOU'LL GET HIT BY A CAR!" do I, in that moment, feel loved? How would I interpret this event? What meaning would I assign to it in my fragile, formative paradigm of life? Would I feel reassured that someone is watching out for me? Or would I think I did something wrong?

Would I think, "It must not be OK for me to be carefree and happy"?

After hundreds or thousands of similar experiences, isn't it possible that I might come to believe my happiness is not important, or that I am, in some undefined way, flawed, undeserving and unworthy of happiness?

How many of these messages, each validating and reinforcing the others, did I receive growing up? How many over the course of my lifetime? But does frequency of repetition equal truth? Does a lie cease to be a lie, just because it's been told ten thousand times? Can I re-examine my beliefs and reform them, based on new understanding? Is it possible to reinterpret my personal story, and in the process, discover new possibilities and new purpose for my life?

So if the belief systems passed down to me have the potential to be either inaccurate or incomplete, and if my past experiences are actually not experiences at all, but rather a malleable mix of interpretations subject to revision, how can I discover what IS true?

Could the question of *why* I believe something be just as important as *what* I believe?

Until I understand the "Why," how can I ever have confidence in *any* "What"?

What's the difference between "Scientific Method" and "Faith Method"? Doesn't it come down to either (a) continuously questioning and challenging, experimenting, testing and ultimately revising, versus (b) voluntarily surrendering my right to question? Doesn't scientific method start from the presumption of incomplete knowledge, open to learning and growth? And doesn't faith method's certainty of conviction preclude consideration of anything that does not fit the predetermined answer set?

But how can I possibly test every question?

Even if I'm willing to provisionally accept the current conclusions put forth by the scientific community and grant that the process of ongoing challenges driven by endless self-interest must distill some measure of truth, isn't it possible, even probable, based on history, that some new discovery, experiment or interpretation may, at any moment, upend one or more of the cornerstones upon which many of my beliefs are founded?

After all, didn't most doctors, in the early 20th century, advocate the notion that cigarette smoking was good for us? Weren't astronomers of the same era convinced there were canals on Mars, indicating the presence of intelligent and organized life? Didn't physicists used to accept as fact that the universe was in a "static state" until analysis of the "red shift" showed that it's expanding? And what happened to the widely held belief that a super volcano killed off all the dinosaurs when that massive asteroid crater was found in 1991? Shall we look for it in the "aether"?

What about the "other questions"?

What about the questions science is not even designed to address, such as: "What's my purpose for being?" or "What is happiness?" or "What is Love?" Where do I look for these answers?

Is this all just some never-ending circle jerk, or is it really possible to discover truth? Is there even such a thing as objective truth?

What if there is and what if it *is* possible to know it?

How would adopting the mindset and acquiring the skills required to pursue truth at this level change my life? How would the quest itself shape my perspective and understanding? Could it help define—or redefine—my values, my sense of security, my perception of worth and beauty, my experience of love, my purpose and direction in life, my ability to find happiness? How might it influence my experience of *everything*?

How would I approach the challenge of discovering truth?

Would I just accept what feels right in the moment, go always with my gut? Or, would I dial up my cynicism and rely solely on critical analysis and rational logic? Heart or head, feelings or facts, Kirk or Spock?

What if these aren't the only choices?

What if both, in some measure, are valid methods of discovery and understanding? What if neither, by itself, is complete? What if what's required is a balance of the two, a symbiotic system for seeking truth?

How can I find this balance? How do I align my intuition with my intellect? How can I learn which to trust, and when?

Chapter 2

TRUST

Don't I, at some point, have to arrive at a "first question"? Don't I need at least one point of reference, a "North Star" from which to navigate? Doesn't it, by definition, need to be my capacity to trust, to make a distinction between what is and what isn't real?

How can I learn to trust my "truster"?

Was I born with some built-in guidance system, an instinct—whether evolved, divinely infused, or both—to lead me in the right direction? In fact, wasn't my immediate instinct to suckle, to cry, to coo and smile, to observe and process new information into my hours-old framework of reality exactly that?

And how did I learn? Driven by instinct to each new behavior, didn't I keenly monitor the results of every experiential experiment to see what did or did not work? What was I seeking? Wasn't it validation of my instincts? Isn't that what I needed in order to begin to trust myself?

But back then, I was so utterly dependent upon my parents or those who cared for me that I couldn't afford to trust only myself, could I? To survive, I had to trust them, too. Since I had nothing to offer them, didn't I have to trust that they would care for me, feed me, clothe and house me, just because they loved me?

What kind of love is given with no expectation of anything in return?

I arrived pre-programmed to need unconditional love, in the same way my lungs need air. And my parents were pre-programmed from their birth with maternal and paternal instincts that kicked in when I was born. Wasn't my instinct to trust in their instincts the vehicle that allowed me to receive the unconditional love I needed then?

Over time, though, their ability to always be unconditionally loving to me gave way to the pressures of their lives, didn't it? When was the first time I cried to let them know I needed something and instead of unconditional love, I felt his or her frustration or anger? When was the first time I was yelled at or punished for playing too loudly? When did I first start to learn that my parents had feelings, too, and that I could be held responsible for how my actions affected their feelings?

What was the beginning of my uncertainty, for even a moment, that I was worthy of their love? And, in those moments when I felt that unworthiness, how could I continue to trust that they could love me?

If I was unworthy of their love, how could anyone love me? How could I even love myself?

Life has certainly gotten more complicated with each passing year, hasn't it? Soon, it wasn't just about my parents, was it? Siblings, extended family, friends of my parents, pastors, teachers, schoolmates, friends, romantic interests, work relationships, spouses, children—all have their own needs and agendas, don't they? I've had to figure out how much and in what ways I can trust, or must not trust, every other person in my life, haven't I? And I haven't always gotten it right, have I? In fact, haven't I sometimes messed up so badly that I've ended up feeling like I can't even trust myself?

Having felt the letdown of authority's broken promises, the deep hurt of a friend's betrayal and the sharp sting of infatuation's fickle fate, have I not built walls to protect my heart from further disappointment? When did I learn that I had to behave a certain way, dress a certain way, talk a certain way, *be* a certain way in order to feel even temporarily accepted, let alone loved?

When did I learn to not trust?

To what extent has my willingness to trust anew and my confidence in my own discernment about whom I can or cannot trust been damaged by the experiences of my past when I've trusted too much and too soon? How have these pains of the past translated to rigidity in the present? How has this resulted in the reduction of my trust in my own intuition?

While it's certainly true that it's not safe to trust everyone, have I perhaps learned too well the lessons of self-protection and closed myself off from the very thing I need most of all—unconditional love?

Have I learned to blame others for violating my trust? Have I seen myself as their victim, and thus fallen down the rabbit hole of disempowered victimhood? Do I live in that hole even now? How can I ever hope to find truth until I have learned how to let go of that unproductive perspective?

Who gets to decide what it all means?

What if I pause for a moment to imagine my life as a very large book, with each day of my life represented by a page, beginning with my birth and continuing through today? I may have no idea how many pages are left, but all the pages representing my future are blank. The events of my life, everything that has happened to me or around me, as well as every action I've ever taken, are recorded as type on each page, printed in indelible ink.

But in the margins all around the printed words, notes have been written in my handwriting—literally millions of interpretations. As I look at my book, I realize that not a single event has ever happened in my life that I did not interpret. In fact, this book is my "life story."

As I review my notes, I can see that, early in my first and second years, I began to build upon past interpretations by referencing previous notes. Day by day, year by year, I can see a kind of continuity building, can't I? Various threads formed and were systematically woven into the tapestry of my life as each thread, each series of related interpretations, became the default filters through which I now interpret new experiences that relate in any way.

When each page is turned, it's sealed. Whatever is printed, or written, on that page remains constant. However, the threads of my interpretations continue from page to page, forming my values and my system of beliefs about the world and my relationship to it.

For the most part, the printed portion of each page is irrelevant because I don't actually experience life directly, do I? In fact, every experience I've ever had has come to me indirectly, hasn't it? It may have first come through my senses, but then it was converted to a series of electrical impulses in my brain.

Once any experience or sensation entered my brain, it was then subjected to scrutiny to determine its meaning. After all, I had to have some way of knowing whether the image I was looking at was a puppy playing in the yard or the grill of a Greyhound bus bearing down on me at high speed, didn't I?

So every instant of my experience has been directed through this complex web of interpretive filters, all based originally in instincts hard-coded in my DNA, but progressively, as I grew older, based on my previous set of interpretations. These "reference points" together comprise the most powerful meaning-making machine that's ever existed—my mind.

Does this mean there's no way to change? Am I trapped in a context of my own making, forever a slave to the judgments of my past?

Isn't that up to me?

Today's page is still being written, isn't it? Even though I may be unable to rewrite the pages of my past, don't I have the complete freedom to review any of those past handwritten notes in the margin, to examine how it's been working for me, to consider the fruit it's been bearing in my life? Isn't it within my power to consciously reframe and reinterpret any current event or anything from my past on today's page?

Could this ability to intentionally assign new meaning to past events, to reinterpret my past interpretations, thus redirecting their impact on my future, in fact, be the closest thing to real magic anyone can ever access?

What will I do with my newfound magical powers?

What events will I reinterpret? What past judgements have been blocking me from the quality of life I want now? What self-limiting beliefs will I find to be unsustainable? What new possibilities will open up for me as a result of releasing myself from those limits?

Who have I been rejecting in my life, just because they remind me in some way of a painful past event? What relationships do I have the power to heal? Who will I forgive? Who am I willing to become, if I don't have to be who everyone else expects me to be?

So what have I learned about trust?

Isn't it always linked, in some way, to my most basic need—the need to feel unconditionally loved, to feel valued just because I exist? Isn't that where it all started? Isn't that a logical place to look for an understanding of how to rebuild my trust, to relearn how to "trust my truster"?

Chapter 3

LOVE

Even though my parents may have intended to, may have done their best to, may have believed with all their hearts that they did, unconditionally love me, there were many times when I failed to trust in their love, weren't there? And there were other times when I *was* trusting, and they were simply unable, in that moment or in that circumstance, to be completely loving with me, weren't there?

When that loving connection was broken from either side, how did I feel?

How can I even put words to that feeling? Isn't this a pain I first felt before I even had words? Before my earliest memories? Hasn't this pain always been a part of me? Or is it a pain that started so early in my life that it just seems like a part of me?

How could I, as a tiny child, make any sense of anger coming from my Mom or Dad? Didn't they seem to me, back then, to be gods? Weren't they my sole source of everything, the providers for all my physical needs, the givers of love and caretakers of my emotions? Weren't they the center of my whole universe?

When they told me anything, they had to be right, didn't they? Even when they told me I was wrong? But when they ignored me, that was the worst, wasn't it? How could I be sure I even existed, or deserved to exist, when they turned away from me?

Of course, as I moved from infancy into childhood, I did begin to question them, and even challenge them, sometimes, didn't I? But that just brought more anger, and more assertions that I was wrong, didn't it? Whenever they were pleased with me, it felt so good; but when they were upset or angry, it felt like my whole world would collapse, didn't it? But even though I did my best to learn how to please them, I couldn't always make them happy, could I? Can I even remember how hard I tried? Can I remember how devastating it felt when I tried my best, and still failed?

That's when the resentments started, wasn't it?

If I couldn't make them happy, no matter how hard I tried, then I couldn't trust them, could I? Or, was it that I couldn't trust myself? Or, maybe it was that I simply wasn't good enough? That I was somehow flawed or broken, that I didn't deserve their love? Could it be that I just wasn't worth the effort? When did I first consider that possibility? And when did I first realize that it was more than a possibility?

Coming to that conclusion hurt me deeply. That particular pain was too much, wasn't it? Even though, in my efforts to protect myself, I sometimes pretended it didn't matter whether anyone loved me or not, that wasn't really true, was it?

When I couldn't bear that pain, what did I do?

What could I do? I couldn't make them love me, could I? Or, could I?

I learned early on that people would act like they cared about me if I did what they wanted, what they expected of me, didn't I? How old was I when I discovered I could get grown-ups to give me praise if I smiled at them? Or entertained them? Or told them what they wanted to hear?

When did I learn I could force them to pay attention to me by screaming and throwing a tantrum? How did I discover adults would give me candy or cookies or money as a reward for getting good grades? When did I figure out that I could at least feel safe if I learned to just go along to get along? And if these things weren't real, unconditional love; if they turned out to be just temporary substitutes for what I really craved; if they were nothing more than "imitation love," they still felt better than nothing at all, didn't they?

That horrible feeling of being out of control, unable to do anything to relieve the pain of my emptiness was the worst, wasn't it?

With imitation love, I could at least have some control, right?

I could earn praise, manipulate or use force to gain a sense of power, access many forms of pleasure or hide out to feel safe, couldn't I? And I learned a whole range of behaviors that I could draw upon, as needed, to get my fix of imitation love, didn't I? When I discovered particular ways of controlling others that seemed to work for me, I went back to them over and over, forming patterns of behavior that became habits and eventually became part of my personality.

They're still with me now, aren't they? What are my "go to" methods of taking imitation love when I feel empty and afraid? What are some of the ways I modify my choices to please others so they'll like me? Do I seek their sympathy by regaling them with my tales of woe, always playing the victim? Or, do I get angry and attack those who provoke me?

Am I the person everyone treats with kid gloves because they know I have a short fuse? Do my friends and family sometimes speak knowingly about my bad temper? Or am I the meek wallflower who never takes a stand, who settles for surface level contact with others, who avoids not just conflict, but connection, because I've been so deeply hurt in the past that it just feels safer, now, to keep my own company than to deal with the risks of close relationships?

Has "imitation love" become my default setting?

If I wasn't even worthy of unconditional love from my own parents, why would I think anyone else could ever love me? And if I was *that* unlovable, how could I trust anyone who ever said they would love me, or be my friend, or care about me?

And it turned out just that way, didn't it? Who was the person who first professed to be my best friend, but then turned his or her back on me? Who was my first romantic relationship who later left me feeling betrayed and broken-hearted? All the thoughts I ever had about there being something fundamentally wrong with me just kept getting validated by my experiences, didn't they?

So what did I do? Did I just retreat further into the behaviors that provided me the distractions and brought me the imitation love I've learned to depend on? What else could I do? Haven't I been doing my best, every day, to simply cope with my feelings of emptiness, unworthiness and fear?

What if there's another choice?

What if I could reliably access the real, unconditional love I've always wanted? What if there was a simple way I could get filled, and stay filled, with that love, even to the point of overflowing, giving my love without condition to others around me? What if I never had to feel empty or afraid again? How would that change my life? Wouldn't that make it easier to trust? Wasn't my feeling of not being unconditionally loved the reason I stopped trusting in the first place?

To feel loved like that, I would need to know that someone accepts me just as I am, wouldn't I? That someone would have to be able to accept my imperfections, because I do have them, don't I? As hard as I may try to look like I've got it all together, I'm not really perfect in all ways, am I? Even admitting that to myself requires courage, doesn't it?

32

Haven't I spent my whole life trying to figure out how to measure up to other people's expectations, to look good enough to earn their affection? In one way or another, hasn't nearly every day of my life been spent trying to please someone—my parents, my teachers, my friends, my boss, my spouse? Didn't I learn at a very young age that I'd get into trouble if I didn't do what they wanted, if I didn't *be* who they wanted me to be?

So I learned to put on my mask, didn't I?

I learned to fit an image, to look like what they expected. At some level, I guess I realized it would be impossible to meet everyone's expectations, but there was always someone, or some group, whose approval I could gain, wasn't there?

Did I have the talent, the aptitude and the desire to make it as the good kid, the smart one, the prettiest or the most athletic; or did I feel the harsh sting of others' criticism and disappointment early on, and decide that it would just be easier to fit in with the misfits?

Yet, wherever, and however, I found to feel like I belonged, it came with its own set of expectations, didn't it? To earn the approval of others, I've always had to wear a mask, haven't I?

Is approval the same as acceptance?

Isn't approval really about their liking me because I do what they want me to do, because I please them; where acceptance is about someone caring about me, with no preconditions? Could there ever be anyone who would love me just for being me?

If I truly believed there was someone who could love me like that, wouldn't it be a huge relief to just be real, to let them see me as I am, knowing they would accept me, no matter what truth about me I might reveal?

What if there *are* people like that, lots of them, all around me, offering their love day in and day out; but because of my distrust, I haven't been able to see them? What if I'm standing right beside the 50,000 watt radio tower of love, but I have my love radio turned off? Can I learn how to switch it on?

Can I learn how to receive the unconditional love I so desperately need in my life?

Wouldn't the logical first step be to learn what real love is? Could the love I crave be as simple as knowing that someone truly cares about my happiness without expecting anything in return? How would I find such a person?

What if that's part of the problem, that I've been looking for just one person who can give me all the love I need and *make* me happy? If I set aside all the propaganda of popular culture and really think about it, doesn't that seem unrealistic?

What if I were to shift my thinking about love and start looking for lots of people who could each sincerely care about me just a little? Of *course* I want a primary relationship at some point, a special someone with whom to share the intimacies—the "into-me-you-sees"—of life, and maybe that person is already in my life, but is it fair to crush them with the burden of being my sole source? Could it be that the working formula is to first learn how to fill my heart with some love from many sources? Wouldn't my primary relationship have a better chance of working out if I wasn't so needy?

What would that look like? Do I have any friends who are able to accept me even when I make mistakes? Could I find others like them? What if I started watching for people who seem to be more accepting in general, people who don't spend a lot of time judging others? What if I made a point of getting to know those people?

Will they be easier to find if I start setting aside some of my own judgments, if I choose to be less concerned about how like me they are; about their age, their gender, their ethnicity or their social status; and be more focused on how they show up in the world? Are they open and friendly? Do they seem to be happy? Do they talk more about ideas and interests than about what's wrong with someone else? Do they seem able to forthrightly admit their own weaknesses and failings, without lapsing into victimhood?

If I know someone like that, or if I meet someone new who seems to be that kind of person, how can I find out if they're willing to accept me with my imperfections? Could it be as simple as casually telling them about one of my small mistakes to see how they'll respond? And if they accept me, even with that flaw, wouldn't that mean they're willing to care about me and see value in me, even though I'm not perfect?

Is that something I could build upon, gradually telling them more of the truth about me, progressively letting them see me more clearly as I get to know them better, receiving their acceptance and experiencing their unconditional love? What would it mean in my life to have a friend like that? What would it mean to surround myself with many friends like that?

Who gets to decide if I can make this my reality?

Who's in charge of looking for people who have the potential to become sources of love in my life? Who needs to set a clear intention for this to happen? Who will need to renew and affirm that intention every day, and take specific action to turn that intention into reality? What's that saying, "If it's to be, it's up to me"?

What am I willing to change in my habits or patterns of behavior, what am I willing to give up to create a new, loving reality? Could I begin the process of filling my life with real, unconditional love just by investing two or three hours a week in connecting with new people? What can I learn from them that may lead to a deeper understanding and experience of love in my life?

What practical steps will I need to take to find these people? How many am I looking for? How many may already be among my acquaintances? Where else can I look?

Are there groups of people formed for the purpose of getting to know each other at this level, existing communities I could simply plug in to? What would happen if I looked up real love on an internet search engine?

What am I willing to change in my life to find abundant sources of unconditional love? What am I willing to risk?

The idea that I have to allow myself to be seen with my hidden flaws, weaknesses and imperfections in order for someone to accept me as I am and unconditionally love me is kind of scary, isn't it? And yet, how could it be otherwise? How could I ever know, for sure, that anyone's acceptance and love is unconditional unless I take off my masks and let them see me as I am?

Can I imagine, or perhaps remember from some past similar experience, what that small unit of unconditional acceptance would feel like? Wouldn't it be a lot like love?

Isn't love the opposite of fear, in the same way light is the opposite of darkness?

In fact, isn't it true that there's really no such thing as darkness? Isn't darkness just the absence of light? What happens when I bring light to a darkened room? Doesn't darkness always dissipate in the presence of light? Isn't it the same way with fear? Isn't fear, no matter how profound or entrenched, just the absence of love? Doesn't more love eliminate more fear in the same way more light chases out more darkness?

So as I get to know more and more people who are able to accept me, and as I share many truths about myself with them, I will feel accepted and loved by them, won't I? Even as I imagine it now, I can feel the warmth of that love, can't I? How much richer and fuller will it be when it becomes more than imaginable, but actually tangible?

And what will I feel toward them, my circle of treasured friends? That will be love, too, won't it? And when my heart is filled with that love, I can finally let go of that bitter old lie that I was ever unlovable, can't I? I'll be able to see the truth, then, that just because someone else, no matter who it was, did not have the capacity at that point in their life to love me, my worthiness of being loved and happy was *never* in question, was it? Otherwise, how could my friends love me now?

How does love relate to my search for Truth?

By learning to seek out people who have love to give and allowing them to unconditionally love me, I will have learned how to trust again, won't I?

And I will have discovered that I am, by definition, always a *subjective* interpreter, and as such, I must approach my search for universal truth with a "clean lens" to avoid undue

37

emotional distortion of the information I'm interpreting. Since the absence of love in my life would, like the absence of air in my lungs, result in a debilitating pain impossible to ignore, it's obvious, is it not, that having love in my life is vital to the quality of all my other observations?

And isn't it also interesting that my willingness to tell the truth about the very things I've spent my life trying to hide would lead me back to a capacity for trust—fractured in my youth, now re-emergent as a mature and powerful tool—that would become the foundation for my ability to receive and give love; and thus turn out to be an essential link to seeking truth in all other ways?

Chapter 4

INTELLECT

It's all good and fine to embark on this quest for great, eternal truth, but where am I supposed to look? And how? And how will I know it when I find it? Now that I've learned that careful, responsible trust is a prerequisite for experiencing love, and sufficient love in my life is essential to clear, undistorted interpretations of my experiences and observations, *as well as* the capacity for growing and maintaining more trust, it seems I've circled all the way back to the original "how-to" question of intellect versus intuition, doesn't it?

So what is this thing called intellect?

Was the scope of my intellect set at birth, an immutable product of my genetics; or, is my intellect today the result of everything I've learned? If I had followed a different path in life, if I had been born to a different culture, or a different time, but with my same DNA, would my mind have worked the same as it does here and now? Are some people just luckier than others with respect to intellect, or can anyone learn anything, given enough motivation, commitment and time?

Is my intellect just my ability to think? How do I distinguish it from my ability to feel? Are they really separate?

Am I not capable of thinking about my feelings? And don't I sometimes have a strong emotional response to certain ideas or patterns of thought?

If I'm not clear about whether I'm responding to a particular circumstance or piece of information with my intellect or my intuition, how can I know that I'm using either effectively? Plus, isn't it generally held that they are separate and distinct?

What if I choose to look at each of them through its own, individual lens for now and reserve the right to reconsider the question of their integration later?

One thing's for sure—science seems to be a completely intellectual enterprise, doesn't it? And science seems to be the source of so much knowledge that we can hardly question it, can we? But then, isn't questioning what science is all about?

Wasn't science pretty much developed to bring some balance to the relationship between intellect and intuition?

Before the advent of science, didn't what then passed for intuition rule the roost? Without the structure and organization science brings, intellect really had no ability to stand up to superstition masquerading as intuition, did it? But the dawn of science changed all of that, didn't it?

Actually, what do I know about science? Was I the kid who loved science, couldn't get enough of it, the Brainiac who was always dreaming up some new experiment to enter in the Science Fair? Or, was I the one who hated science, absolutely *knew* I would never, in my adult life, need to know the names of remote constellations, the life cycle of anaerobic bacteria or how to multiply square roots, and was always trying to find some way to ditch science class?

What role has science played in my life?

Am I grateful for the advances in technology that are continually reshaping our world, addressing needs in medicine, communications, transportation and all sectors of society, endlessly altering the way we do just about everything? Or, do I fundamentally distrust anyone who suggests humans are just one more species of animal, evolved from less complex forms of life in an apparent

42

contradiction of the second law of thermodynamics, soulless and godless? Do I secretly suspect one of them might accidently blow up the world one of these days, while they're all playing with their chemistry sets and supercolliders?

What do I *need* to know about science? Aren't there professionals taking care of these things? Isn't my life challenging enough, and then some, without having to worry about what a bunch of geeks are growing in their petri dishes?

How is science relevant to my search for truth, peace and happiness?

As I think about it, isn't science, in its most basic form, just a systematic way of asking questions and seeking answers? Why, then, is it so controversial? Is science just another thing humans do, with the outcomes, whether good or bad, a direct reflection of the people, with their all-too-human values and motivations, behind the activities? Or is it something more?

What is "scientific method"?

Is there something special about an approach to asking questions that starts with observations, forms hypotheses, subjects them to rigorous experimental testing, continuously challenges its own results, publishes its findings to encourage the efforts of others who would debunk them and refers to repeatedly validated and confirmed findings as "theories"? Is there inherent value in a system built around the premise of avoiding presuppositions while ruthlessly seeking every incremental scrap of truth, then organizing those scraps in the most logical way I can?

What is logic and why is it so important in the first place?

Wouldn't one (logical) way to answer that be to consider what life would be like without logic? How could my mind function with no logical points of reference or organizational framework? How could I ever be able to make sense of anything around me, or feel certain that I was safe in any moment? How could I feel anything but terror? And without logic, and science, and the societal progress—agriculture, medicine, civilization and defensive systems—they've brought, isn't it likely that my terrors would be entirely justified?

Is logic, then, simply the way my mind analyzes and organizes information, comparing it with the best knowledge I already have, or can obtain, in my search for truth? Isn't logic a tool I can use to help assign appropriate meaning to the events in my life, writing the most accurate and truthful interpretations in the margins of my "life story book" that I can? And since my intellect seems to inherently have the ability to postulate logical arguments, doesn't it seem logical that I should routinely use this ability, and not just use it, but consciously work to improve it? Actually, isn't that exactly what I'm doing right now?

So how can I best use my natural logic and the disciplines of science in my quest for understanding?

Do I have to be some kind of an expert in order to use scientific method? Isn't it just a matter of remaining open in my thinking, avoiding the traps of dogma and doctrine by being willing to challenge and critique any and all conclusions, equally employing my creativity to the exploration and examination of each logical construct? If I'm sincere in my search, wouldn't I want to be doing that, anyway?

What kinds of questions should I be asking? How should I frame my questions? What if I ask what I think is the most basic question I can about a topic, and later think of another one that's even more fundamental in that area? How can I keep from letting my ego become attached to my hypotheses and conclusions? Isn't it natural to grow a kind of vested interest in something if I've taken lots of time sorting it out? Why does this feel like a lot of work?

Is it really a lot of work, or is it just unfamiliar territory?

Could it be that I'm actually embarking on what will turn out to be a great adventure, but I'm still getting used to the feel of being outside my comfort zone?

If I am just launching my ship on the sea of intellectual inquiry, is it possible that I might learn something about how to navigate by studying the methods used by other explorers who came before me? How have they approached the foundational questions? What biases have they had to overcome? How successful have they been in doing so? What biases—theirs and mine—must I overcome, and what can I learn about that process from their struggles?

But does that mean I must now take their conclusions at face value?

Is there an appropriate balance to be found between starting with the cumulative base of existing knowledge and being willing to question everything? How can I process so much information?

Isn't there now a consensus about the foundational pieces? Don't most scientists agree on such things as the big bang being the origin of the universe, evolution being the mechanism by which life emerged and progressed, black holes, cosmic background radiation, string theory, etc.? There really aren't any big questions left in physics or biology, are there?

Or are there?

What about the ongoing quest for a "theory of everything," a "Grand Unification Theory" to bridge the messy mathematical gap between the macro and the nano scales—the warped space, wormholes and gravitational folds of Einstein's relativity and the too-weird-for-words world of quantum mechanics? And what about that place, somewhere in the middle, the practical, Newtonian world in which we all live and struggle to earn our daily bread?

Could it be that science is not quite so settled in its conclusions as we've been led to believe?

While the whole world seems focused on the development of new technologies, are there, perhaps, as-yet unexplored possibilities or paradigms remaining to be discovered in the most revered corners of our collective consciousness?

How am I supposed to wrap my mind around all of this? And unless I'm a professional scientist, how could I ever hope to have the ability to separate fact from fiction in such a complex and convoluted set of controversies? What could possibly give me the right to challenge or critique the work of such giants as Einstein, Bohr, Feynman and Hawking?

Then again, if one of the core tenants of science is that *everything* is *always* subject to further questioning; and if I am to truly accept responsibility for my own understanding, how could it be otherwise?

Of course, I can read books and watch videos that explain the views of the giants, can't I? And can't I also read the writings or watch the videos of those who offer differing views? Regardless of the specific subject, don't all the proponents of different positions seem so confident, so

46

assured of their rightness, so elegant in their equations and eloquent of speech that sorting out what I am to believe seems an overwhelming task? While logic is a tremendous help, isn't it still too big? Is there some additional tool I can use to discern the truth?

Chapter 5

INTUITION

How do scientists come up with the ideas they so rigorously pursue with all their scientific disciplines?

What is it that causes a lab tech or a professor to one day stop in his or her tracks and say, "Hey, what about this?" What is it that leads them to sometimes feel they're totally wasting their time, chasing wild geese; while at other times having such a sense of certainty about a particular direction that they doggedly pursue a path, even in the face of opposition and ridicule, unable to let go no matter how many reasons there might be for them to do exactly that?

How do artists know what to paint or sculpt?

What particular combination of light and dark, shape and form, color and contrast, subject and substance captures the eye of the photographer, and why? Who approves the poet's pace? Who measures the musician's meter? How do we know when to dance and when to let our hearts sing?

When did I last have the experience of "gut instinct" that compelled me in a particular direction? And what price did I pay when I last went against that instinct? When was there a time I met someone and instantly knew this was *not* someone I could trust? Likewise, what memories do I have of sensing good will in another human being, of somehow knowing, "this person could become a friend"?

How can I define something as personal, subjective and ephemeral as intuition?

Is it "just a feeling" I get sometimes? Is it an emotion, or is it something far deeper, a kind of "natural knowing" that kicks in when I need it? But does it, always? Aren't there times when I desperately want its guidance, but can't seem to find it anywhere? Don't my emotions sometimes get in the way and confuse my intuition's message? Do I sometimes intentionally ignore it because I don't want to hear what my "little voice" is doing its best to tell me?

Beyond defining intuition, how can I learn to trust it? How can I learn to call it out, or more precisely, tune it in, when I need it? What if that's not how it works?

What if my intuition is actually *always* on, but I'm the one who hasn't been listening?

What if I could change that? How can I learn to stay tuned in, to remain connected with my little voice? Could it be as simple as paying attention? Am I able, in this moment, to close off all distractions, go inside my own consciousness and listen, really listen? What does my intuition tell me about trusting my intuition right now?

As I listen for my little voice, am I able to hear that part that says, "Welcome home, I've been waiting for you"? Can I hear the comfort in that voice, the assurance that all it wants, all it has ever wanted, is what's best for me?

Can I distinguish that part that is pure, that part that is really me, from all the other voices screaming for my attention? How can I know which is which? How can I separate out the voices of my parents, my teachers, my past beliefs and interpretations, my own victimhood and self-pity, my ego?

What if I consciously identify all those whose language is based in "should haves," "would haves" and "could haves," and simply set them to the side, for now, along with all their blame, shame, guilt and regrets? I guess I can always go back and pick them up again later, if I really miss them, right?

If I find myself struggling to let go of all those other screaming voices, what can I do? What if I reach out to some people who I know are able to unconditionally love me and ask for their support? Could that connection with external sources of love possibly help me connect with my own inner reserve of self-love?

Isn't that really what my little voice represents?

Can I, by opening myself to unselfconsciously receive their love, turn up the volume of my little voice? As I step further into my relationship with those who love me, will I be able to experience an empathic connection through which I can add their natural knowing to my own?

Is there an even deeper well I can reach into with my intuition, a universal consciousness with which I can align my heart and mind to tap into the source of all natural knowing? Is there a "peaceful presence" that can help me validate that source? How can I learn to identify that presence? Isn't it likely that I will find it much easier to recognize when I develop the habit of regularly quieting the competing noises and voices through meditation and other mindfulness practices?

What am I likely to hear when all the noise has been cleared?

Is it an actual voice, or is it a kind of resonance, like a musical discord resolving to harmony? How can I know when I am in tune? Is it as simple as waiting for that sense of peace, of calm assurance in my heart?

Can I use the presence of this feeling as a kind of navigational system in my daily life?

Could it be that I am actually free to choose my own level of inner awareness at all times, in *every* now moment, no matter what the circumstances? Could it be that my intuition, my natural knowing, always has a deeper understanding of the underlying reality of any situation in my life than I can access with my conscious mind alone and that, as a result, whatever activity I may be engaged in, goal I may be pursuing or game I may be playing will *always* be won or lost at the point of consciousness?

But what if my old beliefs and interpretations are so deeply entrenched that I cannot let them go?

What if I don't want to let them go? What if I'm so invested in a belief I've long held that my intuition seems to be telling me my very identity will fracture if I consider any other option? Is that the kind of thing my intuition would say to me? Could it be that such a message is not really from my intuition, but instead is based in fear of change? Haven't I already seen that fear is simply the absence of love? So, to whom can I reach out in order to fill my heart with love so that I can have the courage to challenge my current convictions and cherished beliefs? After all, unless I'm willing to reach into the deepest recesses of my belief system and hold each piece up to the light, how will I ever know that I am committed to living a life based in truth and not lies?

How does all of this relate to intellect, logic and scientific method? If my intuition is so reliable, why do I even need to constantly question everything?

Can't I just listen to my inner voice and trust it to guide me to every truth I need?

But that would be like tying off one of my own arms or legs, or blinding one of my own eyes, wouldn't it? Aren't intellect and intuition equally important, and actually symbiotic in function? Isn't it like how having two legs allows me to walk, or having two eyes allows me not just to see, but also gives me depth perception? What if I look at intellect and intuition not as separate, competing modalities, but rather as the two synergistic parts of a system that allows me to see much deeper into reality than either could, on its own?

Can I follow the guidance of my intuition to appropriately frame the next question, design an experiment or interpret a data set in my scientific research? Can I strengthen my intuition by calling it to question with logic, challenging it to remain open to the new discoveries of rational process?

Can I simultaneously honor each approach by seeking balance between them?

Can I use one to fill the gaps the other may encounter? Can I choose to trust and use both, ignoring the one-eyed naysayers on either side who sanctimoniously maintain their claim of exclusive rightness while decrying the wrongness of all others?

Thus equipped with trust, love, intellect and intuition, am I now ready to explore the essential nature of reality?

Chapter 6

REALITY

What is real? Does reality consist only of all the things I can see, touch or smack with a hammer?

Is the ability to weigh or measure something the ultimate standard of its existence? Does tangibility equal reality? Am I, and everyone I know and care about, just stuff, moving mounds of matter that can be broken down into piles of elements, calculated in a series of basic ratios, to be sold off by the pound?

Other than the complexity of how I'm organized, am I fundamentally any different from the dirt I walk on? And if the difference *IS* organization, how did that organizational difference come to be? What is life? How could something as extraordinary as life have arisen spontaneously from the chaos and clutter of non-life? And what about other intangibles, like beauty, love, creativity and consciousness? Am I to deem these unreal, just because I can't stuff them in a jar and screw a lid on it?

Likewise, am I quite certain that what I do see, hear, smell, taste or feel is, in fact, real?

Isn't it true that I have never really experienced anything directly, but rather that every physical event in my life has actually been converted by my sensory organs into electro-chemical impulses and transferred via dedicated nerve fibers to specialized parts of my brain, where those impulses are compared with whatever past sensations may reside in the database of my memory and *interpreted* as to their possible meaning to me, at least in part on the basis of judgments I have previously made regarding those past sensations, whether pleasurable or painful?

Also, haven't scientists found that the model my brain uses to form these interpretations is often unreliable? For instance, when I look at the full moon rising, just above the horizon on a crisp October eve, is it not obvious that the moon is far larger than it looks just two hours later, when it has climbed well into the sky? If I am to believe my senses, wouldn't I necessarily conclude that the moon shrank? Isn't there an abundant supply of such examples, where optical, auditory and other sensory illusions fool my mind into thinking something is real that's not? Isn't this the magician's stock in trade? He didn't *really* saw that pretty girl in half, did he?

Beyond illusion, aren't my interpretations constrained by my past judgments?

Didn't Pavlov's dogs develop a physiological response to the sound of a bell based on their conditioning? Haven't lab rats been trained to forego food to the point of near starvation by the cruel application of associated pain stimuli? Is it such a stretch to imagine that the emotional pains of my past may play a role, not only in my current decision-making processes, but even in my perceptions? And if my perceptions are compromised, how does that affect my interpretations?

How can I deal with what I don't know I don't know?

But beyond these intuitively recognizable limitations, isn't there a whole other layer of variance between my perception of physical reality and what is actually real? Haven't scientists now demonstrated that even the most solid steel anvil is actually comprised of microscopic metal molecules, themselves made up of iron and carbon atoms, which have been proven, beyond reasonable doubt, to consist almost entirely of empty space, nominally occupied by infinitesimal bits of whirring energy popping into and out of existence in an uncertain and essentially unknowable quantum frenzy? And yet, if I take this assertion at face value and decide to jam my hand straight through all that empty space, isn't it predictable that pain will become my physics teacher?

So if physical reality is not all there is, what else is there?

Is there a God and if so, who is He and what's He like? Do I have a soul and if so, what's it like? Is there life after death? Is my soul eternal? What about "near death" experiences? Was there life before life? Reincarnation? Are there angels and demons? Are there supernatural miracles and magic? Ghosts? ESP? Telekinesis? What's the meaning of life—why am I here? How can I know God's will for my life? How do I determine what's good and what's evil? Right and wrong? What is order? What is infinity? If this quagmire of questions has persisted through all of human history, how can I hope to find my way out of it now?

Is the nature of reality even knowable?

Can I ever hope to see, and understand, the whole picture when I live inside the frame? Isn't that my quest? Isn't that the same test I was given at birth? If I approach this question logically, shouldn't I be able to identify a finite answer set? What are the possibilities? Aren't there basically only two? Either the world is as it seems to be, as all of our experience confirms, or everything we think of as real must actually be an elaborate illusion, right?

But doesn't the question itself feel silly? Why, in my every day existence, is this even something I need to think about? Why not just accept what is obviously real and be done with it? After all, aren't we, as a society, way past the questions of our ancestors, who stood on the savannah or huddled near the mouths of caves, pointing at the night sky and inventing Gods to explain the mysteries they saw there?

Hasn't science well and truly answered these questions with the Standard Model?

Hasn't it been tested and retested in every conceivable way and at every possible level, from the quantum to the cosmological? Haven't scientists built telescopes that can see to the farthest reaches of the universe and to the earliest moments of time, and mounted them on mountains and hung them in the sky? Haven't they developed intricate theories to explain mass and matter, then built particle accelerators the size of cities to find the infinitesimal, elusive and yet "massive," bosons that, having now been found, prove, once and for all the supremacy of the Standard Model?

Now that humankind has worked from both ends into the middle, can't I just accept that what seems real *IS* real and be done with it? Aren't the dual bridges, from the cosmological scale on one end of the continuum and the quantum scale on the other, to the Newtonian world of my everyday experience, now sufficiently strong to hold the weight of my belief?

And yet, there are still some fundamental questions that remain unanswered, aren't there? And don't some of those questions raise other questions highly relevant to our inquiry? For instance, how could the entire mass of the universe have exploded into existence, in an instant, out of nothingness? Isn't that, really, the same question, just wearing different clothes, as the challenge our childlike faith faced in middle school: "But who made God?"

Does Goldilocks guarantee God?

Despite the extremes evident all around us, from near absolute zero in the depths of space to the billion-plus degree fiery furnaces of the stars, from free-floating weightlessness just a few dozen miles about the surface of our planet to the crushing, inescapable gravitational pull of black holes in the centers of galaxies; why do we seem to live in a 'Goldilocks' universe, where all the critical factors determining the potential for the existence of life are *just right*?

How did the explosive force of the big bang which, had it been only *one-millionth* more powerful, would have prevented the coalescing of matter into galaxies, stars, planets and us, find the *exact* right balance with gravity?

How does the Strong Atomic Force hold atomic nuclei together, with a power so great that its release can produce massive destruction, but with such a short range that its influence falls off beyond the outer edges of each atom's protons and neutrons?

Why is the resonance frequency that naturally occurs in the center of stars *precisely* the frequency required to facilitate the routine occurrence of what would otherwise be an extremely rare three-way fusion of helium into carbon, thus providing an abundance of that critical chemical component of which we are all made?

What are we to make of the fact that literally *all* of the fundamental physical properties of our universe, which could have been different, are instead perfectly configured for life? Given that so many key factors in the laws of physics require such incredible precision for the universe to even exist as we know it, and for us to exist to observe it, doesn't the notion of "a series of random accidents" strain credulity?

So what's the alternative?

Am I to reject the answers science has so painstakingly pulled out of centuries of observation, hypothecation, experimentation and verification, just because it does not yet have ALL the answers? Am I to revert back to superstitions and religions that simply ignore or outright deny everything science has discovered? Will I teach my children myths and mysteries, as I may have been taught?

Or could there possibly be a third option, one in which the reality we observe IS unapologetically real, and yet there is a higher level explanation for the vexing questions; an explanation accessible only through the combined use of our intellect and intuition?

Could reality actually exist on both a physical and a non-physical level simultaneously?

Don't I have experience that supports the plausibility of such a reality? Haven't I felt the wonder of beauty, the power of inspiration, the essence of love all within the space of my own physical existence, and yet known these things to be beyond tangibility? Haven't I had moments of reflection that left me wondering whether I was a human being having a spiritual experience or a spiritual being having a human experience?

Could we all be living in a kind of multilayered, multidimensional projection?

Is it possible that an unimaginably vast intelligence is experiencing the many different ways there are to be human through us? Rather than highly evolved, yet disconnected animals, each fundamentally alone and on its own, striving to survive in an impersonal, unpredictable and often hostile sea of random materialism, could it be that we are all individual manifestations of one omniscient and omnipotent intelligence who has chosen to express and experience what it means to be human by living billions of human storylines?

Is it true, what Shakespeare wrote, that "All the world's a stage, and all the men and women merely players ..."?

Am I actually an eternal, divine being, living out this life from beginning to end, constrained in my perception and limited to this physical plane, as if this is all there is, *by my own volition*, the better to enjoy the thrill of discovery, the drama of defeat, the victory of overcoming obstacles and the joy of finding love? Could it be that what I experience as reality is simply the tangible (to me) expression of the *idea* of me in the mind of God?

And yet, reality does seem so very real, doesn't it?

But of course, it would, wouldn't it? What would be the point of creating an unconvincing illusion? If I were designing a game to play, and I had infinite resources, time and creative capacity, wouldn't I make it perfect in every way? What detail would I leave out? And if I existed in a realm of infinite possibilities, but with no tangibility, wouldn't the manifestation of some of that limitless potential be a priority? Wouldn't it, in fact, be a *necessity*?

So how can we know? And if we, the players, truly are required to live within a reality constructed by an infinitely powerful manifestor who is really us, then wouldn't it make sense to just accept the reality that apparently is real and do our best to live within it? When it's all said and done, is there any value in this exercise?

Isn't there?

If, in the course of framing these questions and searching for answers, we discover some deeper truth about our connection with others, to the universe in which we live and to our most fundamental selves, will that not have been worthwhile? If we gain an understanding of our personal permanence, a belief in our transcendence over mortality and thus, a larger perspective on life, could that not give us a greater ability to persevere in the face of hardships we may encounter in this life? If we come to see our own handwriting on the wall of the world, might we not have a fuller understanding of our power and creative potential? Is this not extraordinary value?

How can I use my intellect and intuition to discover the answers to these questions?

Doesn't my intuition tell me that the answers must exist, somewhere? Doesn't my intellect suggest that if I can only find a logical starting point, a thread to begin pulling, I may just, with a little determination and a lot of patience, be able to unravel this tangle?

What if, being the clever Creator we would hope we are, we have left clues for ourselves?

What if our basic curiosity about such matters is one of those clues? What if there are more? And what if we've left more than just clues? What if the Creator built into the very fabric of the universe a set of intangible, yet quite real, laws that we, as human beings, can learn to access through our intuitive connection with infinite mind? What if developing a mastery of these laws can be every bit as useful in this life as learning about gravity or radio waves or mathematics?

What is the loose end of the thread I'm looking for? Could it be consciousness?

Chapter 7

CONSCIOUSNESS

What is consciousness? Why, after decades of dedicated research by the best scientists in the business, during which time they have made amazing discoveries about the structure and function of the human brain, does no one have a good answer to the question of consciousness?

Why, after all that time and effort, have they still not even reached consensus on *how to frame the question* of consciousness?

Will researchers someday be able to break consciousness down into a set of component parts and thereby establish the ultimate veracity of the reductionist approach, once and for all? Will they discover a heretofore un-noticed "consciousness gland"?

Or will it be a puzzle, where scientists sitting astride some enormously powerful functional magnetic resonance imaging machines finally finesse from the brain behaviors of various volunteers the obscure neural networks and synaptic sequences that result in my knowing I am me? Will I awake one day to read, as I drink my morning coffee, a posting confirming that I am, in fact, entirely mechanistic and unremarkable, differentiated from the predictability of my coffee maker only by the level of my programming?

How likely is it that we will soon have technologies that allow us to program consciousness into robots? What will happen when they become smarter than we are? Doesn't the computational speed of microchips already exceed that of individual brain circuits by millions of times?

When computers do catch up with our massive multi-processing capabilities, will we find a way to upload our consciousness into machines? Or will they quickly grow tired of supporting us? Will it be Kurzweil's superintelligence singularity or I.J. Good's intelligence explosion? Asimov's Three Laws or the extinction of man? The Jetsons or the Terminator?

Or will the scientists laboring on the front lines of this final frontier continue to encounter, as they have thus far, more mysteries at every turn, each new layer laden with questions more daunting than those that came before? Are they closer to a breakthrough, or a breakdown? Will progress in the science of consciousness finally yield the hoped-for result—irrefutable proof that we are nothing special after all—or might there be some surprises yet ahead on this particular horizon?

Which came first, consciousness or the brain, the observer or the observed?

That's really the foundational question, isn't it? Did we evolve into consciousness, or does consciousness exist independently, outside of our bodies? Is my consciousness something that originates from within me, the natural and perhaps inevitable result of bio-electro-chemical processes going on in the three-pound lump of pinkish gray protein that rides around in a bone box perched above my shoulders? Is it just an adaptation, stumbled upon by natural selection as a survival advantage, maybe even an artifact of some past evolutionary challenge?

Or, does my physical brain merely mirror a much larger awareness, channeling, as it were, the mind of God? Can't I, by first answering this question to my own satisfaction, build a framework in which to address all of those other questions?

Is it even fair to think of consciousness as a strictly human trait? Or is this just one more example of anthropomorphic arrogance? Do other, non-human animals

70

have consciousness? Could it be that they do, but simply lack the ability to describe it in words we can understand?

Haven't scientists discovered that some other species seem to have their own abilities to communicate, albeit different from ours? Haven't some people learned how to read and form rudimentary interpretations of the body language of horses, dogs and even deer? Haven't they shown that they're able to communicate with individual animals and, in fact, demonstrated that these animals have a rich and robust non-verbal language of their own?

Haven't researchers taught apes, whose voices are physically unable to produce human speech, but whose hands are marvelously dexterous, to use human sign language, only to be stunned by the complexity of their thought processes?

Isn't it now generally accepted that dolphins are communicating with each other as they emit their beeps and clicks, and that the whale song filling the oceans is not only beautiful, but purposeful? Haven't we now discovered that elephants routinely communicate over long distances with sounds that happen to be in a frequency range just slightly below what humans can hear with our naked ears?

How many thousands, or tens of thousands, of individuals from these species have humans killed for their own economic interests, without even considering the possibility that these majestic creatures might be aware of their own lives; might have a language with which they express and emote; might have families they care about and social structures in which they live and contribute to their communities? How much carnage have we carelessly inflicted, just because we could not hear their language as we hear ours, and because we neglected to put forth the effort to discover if they might have one of their own?

What are we to make of all this other-species and even trans-species communication? What about the results of research that now indicate some level of self-awareness and even abstract and conceptual thinking by chimpanzees? Does this not rise to the level of consciousness and, if it does, does that support the notion of an evolutionary, and thus, biological explanation for consciousness? Could it not, just as easily, be seen as evidence of a universal consciousness, what some have called, "the One"?

What if consciousness is not an either/or question, but one of magnitude?

What if all living beings possess some degree of consciousness, some less and some more, perhaps, but all with some? What if consciousness is actually a fundamental attribute of life, a definitional characteristic, maybe even THE true distinction between life and non-life? What if consciousness is what has been described in various creation stories as "the breath of life"?

And what if human beings are NOT the ultimate repository of consciousness? What if, like other animals, we, too, are constrained in our capacity for communication with other life forms, such that there may be much higher, even *infinitely* higher concentrations of consciousness of which we remain blissfully unaware? What if, after hundreds of years of scientific exploration, we are forced to admit (at great price to our egos) that we have not learned all there is to learn?

What if, by consciously opening our minds, we come to discover that we have only scratched the surface of all there is to know, not just about matter, energy, time and space, but about the incomprehensively vast intelligence of un-manifest potentiality?

Does consciousness necessarily exist within the domain of physics? Could the inherently subjective limitations in our abilities to see beyond the interests, and current prejudices, of our own species be preventing us from considering the possibility of another realm of reality, in which our universe exists as a component, rather than the totality? Isn't this what string theorists ask us to do, when they talk about all those extra dimensions we can't see?

How might consciousness relate to intelligence at the multi-verse scale?

Is intelligence limited to the familiar framework of time, space, matter and energy? Or, as Einstein and Bohr have posited, is the framework itself to be called into question? What if universal intelligence is more than just a collection of what *IS*, or has been; more than simply a sequential light record of those possibilities that *have been* made manifest? What if universal intelligence encompasses ALL possibilities, including those that have *not yet been* expressed, in this universe, or in any parallel universe?

If intelligence could be defined, at least in part, as an infinite set of possibilities, as a framework of ideas, wouldn't the only parts of that infinite set constrained by the laws of physics be those parts that, within any given moment, have already been expressed within the physical universe?

So who gets to decide which possibilities manifest and which ones remain within the realm of pure potentiality?

What if that's where consciousness comes in? What if it's MY consciousness that determines the expression of one possibility over another? What if *I* am the actuator? What if it's been my hand on the lever all along, and I've never realized it? What if the best definition for consciousness is the *moment by moment experience* of expressing what is out of what could be, of manifesting the material world from the realm of infinite potentiality?

If I pause to consider the logical implications of what I already know, won't I arrive at an inescapable conclusion that I am, as an interactor (through my choices), or even as just an observer, playing an essential role in the manifestation of my reality?

Doesn't the Uncertainty Principle that now serves as a cornerstone for our understanding of quantum mechanics make clear that everything exists as potential until it is observed, and that the act of observing is *never* really passive? Shall we open the box and ask Mr. Schrödinger's cat?

What if the particle physicists are right, that the nature of reality at the quantum level is far stranger than we could ever imagine, that NOW is the only moment we ever actually have, that the universe of just one second ago no longer exists, and the universe of one second from now remains unexpressed until we get there?

What if the sequence of manifestations I experience as the arrow of time is, in the most fundamental sense, actually a series of windows opening within my consciousness, like the frames of a film, but with the seemingly discreet entity I know of as me continuously rewriting the script and redirecting the scenes, with only the most fleeting awareness that I am doing so?

What if I am actually far more powerful than I have ever dared to believe?

What if my beliefs are, in fact, the mechanism by which my consciousness expresses my reality?

What if, as Ernest Holmes said, my belief sets a limit for the expression of a principle, which, of itself, has no limit?

What if the reality I experience in my day-to-day life is, to an extent beyond what I could have ever imagined, the direct result of me exercising my power of choice?

Chapter 8

CHOICE

It's the age-old question, isn't it—predetermination vs. free will? Does God have a plan for my life or am I on my own? What if both are true? Can I see myself living my life, as I always have, trying to figure out what to do in each new situation, generally unable to predict from one day to the next what's just over the horizon; yet simultaneously imagine an intelligence who knows, without controlling, what each frame of my life's film will reveal?

If not, could my imagination be the limiting factor?

How could such an intelligence exist? Isn't intelligence always expressed as thought, and isn't thought the direct result of the sequential firing of synapses in our physical brains? Doesn't anything that happens in sequence automatically fall within the definition of time? How can I conceive of any intelligence existing outside of the framework of time?

And yet, somehow I've managed to live my whole life up to this point taking for granted that the sun will come up each morning and set every night, haven't I? When, as a child, I learned that it wasn't the sun moving after all, but rather that I live on a huge roundish rock, orbiting a giant ball of nuclear fusion at an incomprehensible speed, and that our sun is just one of millions of stars spread out across our galaxy and billions comprising the universe, didn't I find a way to make peace with the references to distances, temperatures, numbers and timespans that exceeded my mind's capacity to grasp?

How long did it take me to accept the premise of an inanimate order to the dance of the planets and moons in our solar system? What pattern of sequential thoughts set this dance in motion? Why is the sky blue? How does light know to split apart into the exact same rainbow of colors every time it encounters a particular combination of water's mist and light's angle? How can I consider these things and not be filled with a sense of wonder and awe? And as I look deeper into each of these phenomena, do I not discover more and more layers of progressively elegant and complex order?

If this is not intelligence, what is?

If, as our understanding of quantum physics would now seem to indicate, the universe is NOT static, but rather, continuously in the process of being *re*-created, atom by atom, instant by instant, wouldn't it be logical to conclude that I must be part of that ongoing creation process? What if, at each moment, there is a vast new set of possible universal configurations that *could* manifest, but only one of which *will* in that instant, thereby closing off forever certain pathways to future manifestation, while leaving open or even increasing the probability of others?

What if the option expressed is determined, in part, by whatever choice I happen to be making in that moment? Wouldn't that mean that, by the simple act of making choices throughout my day, I am literally co-creating the universe into which I will live?

But how does that work? It's one thing to *say* my choices determine the future direction of the universe, but it's entirely another matter to substantiate such a brash claim, isn't it?

What if it's a little like a television screen or computer monitor, where software designed to maximize efficiency analyzes each line of pixels before it's sent to the display, to see which ones need to change and which ones will be left as they were in the previous frame? Could a similar process be happening in three dimensions with elementary particles at a quantum scale?

What if the entire universe is being annihilated and recreated, particle-by-particle, over and over again on a timescale measured in attoseconds*?

What if our choices, mingled with the choices of other people, and other causative factors, provide the energy inputs necessary for change to occur from one iteration to the next? Do I have a better explanation?

Of course, there are many who would simply say this is the hand of God moving in our world, aren't there? But even if that ultimately turns out to be an appropriate description, am I not, in my quest for a deeper understanding, committed to further explore the mechanism? What might that exploration reveal and how might those revelations affect the choices I make in my day to day life?

Could it be (extending the metaphor), that God's hand has many fingers? Could I be one? In fact, could that perhaps be a better description than I realize? If I look at my own hand what do I see? Even though each finger seems to have its own separate identity, it isn't really separate, is it? Isn't each finger part of my hand, and isn't my hand part of my arm, which is, in turn, part of my whole body?

Separate, yet one—could this be the real meaning of "created in God's image"?

As I choose—what to eat, what to wear, where to go, who to talk with, who to be kind to, where to work, who to love,

---

* An attosecond is one quintillionth of a second. According to Johan Mauritsson, an assistant professor of atomic physics at Lund University in Sweden, who helped develop the attosecond laser that made it possible, for the first time ever, to film the movement of an individual electron: *"It takes about 150 attoseconds for an electron to circle the nucleus of an atom. An attosecond is 10^{-18} seconds long, or, expressed in another way, an attosecond is related to a second as a second is related to the age of the universe."* – www.photonics.com

who I am in each now moment—am I not altering the fabric of reality in my corner of the universe?

When I look at the process of creation as dynamic and ever-changing, rather than static and stuck, don't I see the deeper truth that each new moment of my life brings a new set of possibilities awaiting my direction?

If I truly believe in my creative potential, what will I choose to create today? If anything is possible, what limits will I accept?

If I know, beyond any shadow of doubt, that *I absolutely cannot fail*, what challenge will I choose? Likewise, if I come to understand that my choice is *always* a determining factor in what comes next, when will I allow myself to go unconscious and unaware?

What are the constraints on my power to create? If I'm not restricted by a harsh and immoveable static reality, will I be stopped by economics? Will I allow artificial barriers to block my way? The expectations of family members or friends? Of my spouse or boss or partner? Of society in general? What lessons have I learned in my life that I must now unlearn in order to be truly free?

If I am to embrace the radical idea that my choices actually define the future, how can I reconcile that with my past experience? Haven't I found the limitations I've encountered in my past to be all too real? How can I account for my current state of insufficiency if I am, and presumably have been all along, the master of my own manifestation? If I could have chosen whatever life I wanted, why am I not infinitely rich and good-looking? Why am I still struggling to find the formula that will lead me to love and happiness?

How can I make peace with the notion that, *based on results*, I now have exactly what I intended?

Could it be that I have simply misunderstood the mechanism of manifestation? Have I, in fact, been expressing a reality based in my beliefs but, without realizing what I was doing, been sending mixed signals into the machine? If, in one moment, I'm daring to dream, but in the next I find myself descending into doubt; if I am vacillating between love and fear, truth and lies, commitment and holding back; if I am, and have been, a classic collection of opposites, why would I be surprised to find chaos and disorder in my life?

So what's the secret? Surely, I can't just suddenly start manifesting the reality I want in my life, can I? I can't, with a straight face, say that I expect the entire universe to start bending to my will now, can I? What if I can?

What if all of life pretty much comes down to learning how to make the right choices?

What if the key is discovering how to bring my attention and intention to a clear focus, to align my thoughts so that the message I am putting into the machine of unfolding creation is one of consistency?

What if it's about developing the personal discipline to be mindful of my thoughts, to trust that my thoughts will become my reality and to act like it, to finally lay aside my victimhood and confidently claim my role as victor?

Can it be that simple? Can I tap into the power to produce the results I want in my life by simply choosing to own all the outcomes I have already expressed and am now expressing?

Yet, this can be a surprisingly hard pill to swallow, can't it?

To accept full accountability for my life means I have to be willing to acknowledge all the stupid and sometimes cruel mistakes I've made, to be willing to face all the truth I've worked so hard to deny, to admit the times I've managed to shift the blame onto someone else, to see clearly the things I did to make myself look good, often at the expense of others, doesn't it?

Do I really have to suffer such a blow to my ego?

What if it has been my ego that has held me in the captivity of ignorance and resistance? Can't I feel it pulling on me, even now? Wouldn't some part of me rather push aside all the potential power I've been promised in favor of just leaving my life as it is?

Can I, in my mind's eye, segregate that part of me and see it as a separate entity; and just watch as it denies the possibility for positive change and simultaneously decries the price as too high to pay? Can I feel that entity's discomfort, my ego's perceived existential threat?

So who's in charge of the choice I make—the entity I can identify as my ego? Or, is there another, deeper, me in here somewhere?

Isn't my ego just a construct that has emerged from the constant stream of judgments I've been making my whole life? Isn't it the byproduct of my non-stop mental narration of "the story of me," the set of interpretations I originally developed to protect me from the pain of feeling unloved? Isn't it telling me, right now, that even if I could reinterpret my past and redefine myself, it would simply be too much work?

Isn't my ego the part of me that's so sure I'm all alone out here, that I'm not really part of any bigger whole; that God, if God even exists, is somewhere out there, at a very great distance?

Isn't it my ego that has driven all my past choices to build up my image in the eyes of others, to protect myself or to grab a momentary gain? Hasn't it done its best to convince me that being favorably compared with other human beings is the most important thing, the ONLY thing that really matters in my life?

Can I, having seen the truth about my ego, simply choose to *thank it* for looking after me the best it has known how and gently move it to the side so I can look beyond its selfish interests to consider a new, more profound meaning for my life?

Am I willing to step into this new set of possibilities, this *freedom* to demonstrate for myself the power to create different outcomes in my life?

And if I am, where shall I start?

If I consider all that I've learned about truth, trust, love, intellect, intuition, reality and consciousness, can I see that I now have the tools to construct a solid foundation for mindful practices that will enable me to make powerful and responsible choices?

And didn't I hear somewhere that "with great power comes great responsibility"?

Chapter 9

RESPONSIBILITY

When I think of the word "responsibility," what comes up for me? Do I feel a sense of obligation, of needing to "be responsible" because that's what's expected of me and if I'm not, somehow I'll be found out and either punished or horribly embarrassed? Is it one of those words that always seems to be said in a serious, or even stern, voice?

What about the word "accountability"? Does that word send me scurrying for cover? Have I been taught that it is synonymous with "blame," only bigger and badder, as in "Who's accountable for this mess?!" meaning someone's about to get fired?

In exercising my power of choice, how much power do I often give up without even realizing I'm doing so, simply by accepting, without question, the definitions of certain words that have been given to me by others? Could it be a lot? Could it, in some cases, be nearly all? Could the emotional connotation I put on a word, the meaning I unconsciously assign to it because, well, that's how I've always thought of it, ever since I first learned the word; could that feeling I associate with the word actually frame my choice in such a way that I no longer have much of a choice at all?

Whose responsibility is it to decide on *my* definitions for words like "responsibility" and "accountability"? To whom must I account for my decisions?

What if I look more closely at each of these words and consider what they really mean? Can I set aside my history with these words and open my mind to new definitions with brand new, intentionally established emotional attachments?

When I break the word into its component parts, doesn't it become obvious that "response-ability" is about my ability to respond? And that "account-ability" refers to my ability to account for something? It would seem, wouldn't it, that, far from assigning obligation or blame, these two words actually speak to my core capabilities—my ability to respond, presumably in a way that furthers my objectives, ultimately increasing my happiness; and my ability to account for, to understand and to take full ownership of the choices I make and the role each of those choices plays in producing the outcomes I experience?

Do these definitions speak of enslavement, or empowerment? Isn't the ability to respond to whatever life may throw at me the very essence of power? And doesn't having the ability to account for the influence of my choices give me the opportunity to learn lessons from every experience, to grow in my capacity to correlate my choices with the results they are most likely to produce, and thus to elevate my effectiveness?

Rather than "got to do," could it be that responsibility and accountability are "*get* to do"?

What are the fundamental areas of responsibility in my life? If I've always thought of such things as brushing my teeth, making my bed, finding a job, going to work, paying taxes and paying my bills on time as my areas of responsibility, is it any wonder I may have come to resent the whole idea?

But isn't it also my responsibility to choose my direction in life, to decide what I believe in, to determine my values, to identify and pursue my passions, to maintain balance in my life, to discover love, to play and have fun, to find joy? Isn't life an adventure to be lived, a journey to be savored rather than an ordeal to be endured?

Isn't it ultimately up to me, regardless of any outside influences or factors, to choose how I will live my life?

But what about those tasks I simply have to do, whether I want to, or not? Aren't there some true "got to dos" in life? What example comes to my mind now of something I despise doing, but have to do because it's "my responsibility"?

Now, as a little mental exercise, can I say what would happen if I just stopped doing it? Who would I let down? What would fall apart? If I call my doing the dreaded deed "A" and NOT doing it "B," then can I refer to the most direct and attributable consequence of "B" as "C"? And as I consider "C," what would be the likely sequence of follow-on results? Where could this string ultimately lead?

If someone important to me counted on me to do "A," and I disappointed them ("B"), would I lose my job, be seen as a failure, miss an opportunity or betray a friend ("C")? If such a thing were to happen, how would I feel about the consequence ("D")? Could it ultimately bring on feelings of regret ("E"), resulting in withdrawal and isolation ("F"), leading to loneliness ("G"), deepening into depression ("H"), dropping into despair ("I") and finally, after using up all the other letters, ending at hopelessness ("Z")?

Isn't it clear that my real choice was always between "A" and "Z"?

Doesn't that make it easier to see "A" as something I "get to do" instead of a task I've "got to do"? When I really think about it, can't I see that all the responsibilities I face are actually of my own choosing, each one inextricably linked to the quality of life I want and the full measure of happiness I'm pursuing each day?

If, through previous unawareness or unacceptance of the relationship between my choices and my results, I have made a mess of my life to this point, who gets to straighten it out?

Will I waste one more precious minute of my life assigning blame or indulging in the pointless process of trying to change the past?

No matter how trapped I may have felt up till now, don't I have the power to choose, in this moment, a new direction?

While I'm at it, why not also consciously reframe my routine responsibilities as daily or weekly intervals in which I "get to" exercise privileges I may have come to take for granted; privileges other people in other places or circumstances can only aspire to?

For instance, the act of brushing my teeth takes on new meaning when I stop to think how different my life would be if I had lost my teeth, or my ability to use my hands, through injury or disease, doesn't it?

Making my bed is not such a chore, is it, when I realize there are millions of refugees whose beds, if they have any at all, are nothing more than thin mats rolled out on hard ground?

Likewise, the prospect of going to work and paying my bills feels somewhat different when I consider the alternative of not being able to provide for myself and my family, doesn't it? Given these contrasts, my responsibilities don't seem quite so onerous, do they?

Who knew such a simple shift in perspective could so alter my experience of my responsibilities?

But responsibility is not just about shifting perspectives to redefine the direction or reframe the routines of my life, is it? Isn't it also about responding to the challenges I encounter? And my ability to respond to challenges, both big and small, fundamentally depends on my being able to account for the role of my choices in the results of my life, doesn't it?

Does this mean there are no other factors? Have I not had to deal with many circumstances that were completely outside my control?

Am I to accept 100% of the responsibility for every experience in every moment of my life? What would happen if I did?

While it may seem obvious that things happen to me and around me, over which I have no direct control, don't I always get to choose how I will respond to any event or circumstance that arises?

Who gets to write the "meaning in the margin" on today's page of my life story?

What would I need to give up in order to be truly free to interpret the events of my life—past, present and future—in a way that leaves me accountable for all of it?

What would happen if I simply let go of the notion that life must always be fair and that justice must prevail? Could I learn to forgo my habit of looking for excuses and my tendency to assign blame?

Can I face a future in which I no longer reflexively respond to my need to always look good in the eyes of others and even in the eyes of my own ego?

Am I willing to let go of my non-stop judgments of everything and everyone around me?

What if, as the oft-recited prayer suggests, I could be granted "the serenity to accept the things I cannot change, the courage to change the things I can and the wisdom to know the difference"? Could such extreme accountability be the key to my empowerment? Actually, isn't that the whole point of that particular prayer?

When I find within myself the strength to embrace my accountability and claim the freedom it facilitates, what will I do with that freedom? What will I begin to manifest—in my thoughts, in my choices, in my day-to-day interactions, in my relationships with the people I care about, and in my relationship with God?

Chapter 10

GOD

Who, or what, is God?

Is He some gray-bearded giant sitting above us all on a massive, jewel-encrusted throne, dispensing an ultimate justice of which He is the arbitrary arbiter?

Or is He a fiction, a patriarchal fantasy concocted by fearful and ignorant early humans to make sense of phenomena they were unable to explain, soon co-opted by clever and greedy power seekers among them who anointed themselves priests, chosen by Him to communicate His will and collect offerings on His behalf?

Is He to be feared, a God of vengeance who has a history of sending a flood to wash away the unrighteous, destroying disobedient cities by fire, piling plagues and pestilence upon nations whose pharaohs defy His commands and even ordering the indiscriminate slaughter of innocents who had the effrontery to stand in the way of His plans for His chosen people?

Is He the unyielding writer of rules requiring blood sacrifice as atonement for ubiquitous sin? Or is He a loving Father, willing for His only Son to die, so that we might be saved, if we but truly believe?

Is God the Creator of the universe, the Omniscient and Omnipotent, the Alpha and Omega, the Lord of All? Or is He a personal God, someone I can talk to, go to when I need a friend, someone who cares about every detail of my day? Is God active in this timeline, hearing every prayer, weighing every supplication, interjecting Himself into the affairs of men when it suits His will? Does He walk with me in the garden? Is His grace amazing? Is His eye really on the sparrow?

Am I quite certain that He is a "He"?

Could it be that every metaphor we humans have ever invented to describe God is just a grossly inadequate, anthropomorphic construct of our imaginations? Have we had to resort to such limited linguistic tools because the truth is so completely beyond our current comprehension?

Or is that just an excuse for intellectual and intuitive laziness, at a societal level?

How can we justify abandoning such important questions as the existence and nature of a higher, perhaps infinitely higher, intelligence to the priests and preachers of ancient religions who hold themselves and their books as the exclusive and unassailable bearers of truth?

How have we allowed them to position science as the enemy of God? And why have scientists so easily bought into that characterization and the resultant cultural polarization?

Are we really incapable of moving past our historical perspectives and opening our minds to new ways of seeing? Is this another case where the definition of one word has profound significance to the framing of an entire field of investigation? Could we, if we set aside the emotionally charged word "God" for just a moment, conceive of ways we might scientifically approach the search for evidence of another, organizing level of intelligence?

Have we become so cynical and full of ourselves that we simply refuse to recognize the infinite intelligence underlying our very existence?

Can I not see the elegance of mathematics? Am I blind to the intricacy and efficiency of design in every layer of apparent reality, from the quantum to the cosmological?

Do I not find it easier to believe, as Einstein suggested, that everything is a miracle rather than nothing is a miracle?

If I so easily accept that the thumb drive I can hold between my two fingers is an organized system for the storage of information, why would I have difficulty seeing the universe itself as a holographic repository of knowledge?

When I routinely awaken each day to new discoveries in every field of scientific research, why do I struggle with the idea that there may be a bigger game at play than I have yet seen? Doesn't the very act of making new discoveries presuppose something was already there to be discovered? And doesn't that intrinsically infer the bigger game?

How does our understanding of superstring theory and the multiverse fit with the concept of this "bigger game"? Does God love all the various versions of me that might exist in alternate universes just the same? What if some of them are not as nice as I am? What if some of them are liars, thieves or murderers?

Is God's love really unconditional?

How do we reconcile the apparent existence of at least thousands and perhaps billions of habitable planets in this universe with a unique status for humankind? Can we? Or, must we logically accept the possibility that there could be other civilizations far more advanced than ours, perhaps even now sending emissaries or armies toward us at speeds beyond our comprehension? Does our God love them, too?

How does our concept of individual consciousness mesh with the idea of one universal consciousness?

Are we, as previously explored, all individual manifestations of one mind? If this resonates with my intuition as being true at some level, could there be more than one way for this truth to manifest in my reality? Am I willing to consider new ideas I've never heard of or thought of before? Am I, even if doing so takes me far outside my comfort zone?

Where do we land when we project the trend lines for human technological development out hundreds or thousands of years?

What happens when we raise Moore's Law to an exponent of its own magnitude?

When computers become smarter than we are, what will happen to us? Will we be clever enough to create a symbiotic relationship with artificial intelligence?

Will we be wise enough to prepare for that eventuality? If so, shouldn't we be doing that right now?

Are we already in danger of being too late? If we miss that window of opportunity, will we one day wake up to discover that we are just a problem to be solved by a new, higher order planetary regime? Will there be a God to protect us? Or will humanity become a historical anomaly, a critical but subsequently unnecessary link in the evolution of machine intelligence?

If we do manage to find that symbiotic balance with sentient technology, how will we use it?

When I have the ability to upload my memories and personality into a program designed to emulate every relevant function of my brain, will that program become "me"? Will I simply discard my dying body and "switch on" my immortal self? Would I, if my body were racked with disease and I could simply turn off the pain, but continue with my existence? Would I, if I had already died, but had previously made a "backup"?

With a fancy new electronic brain operating at a clock speed many orders of magnitude faster than my original biological model, what will I do to keep from being bored? Will a day seem a million times longer when I can think a million times faster?

Will I continue to build faster and better computers into which I can upload myself? Where will it stop?

At molecular scale? At atomic scale? Can information be stored on photons? Isn't that how *all* information is ultimately stored?

How will I relate to others who have also made the jump from physical to virtual existence? Will we use our newfound capabilities to compete at an ever higher level, devising new ways to wage war, arranging server-crashing "erasure" events for the mass annihilation of those we find undesirable or with whom we disagree?

Or will we, by contemplation of the alternative, finally choose cooperation and collaboration, developing "trust protocols" that allow us to literally share each other's thoughts and experiences? Will we create a new kind of internet, a communications platform that will eventually enable all sentient beings to join together as one functional mind?

Could such a mind, expanding at a geometrically increasing pace, someday evolve to gain mastery over time and space in the same way we have already learned how to convert matter into energy and energy into matter?

By transcending physical death, would we have the luxury of traveling at near light speed throughout the universe, exploring other planetary systems and "seeking out new civilizations, going where no one has gone before"? Or, if we could someday unlock the secrets of time, would we simply "leap" through space and travel through time?

Might we, with unlimited computing power, simply choose to be at all places at all times?

If this all seems too outrageous, too far-fetched, can I start at the objectionable end and follow the rational progression backward until I find a logical stopping point? Where would that be? Can it even be stopped? Why would I want to? Just because it seems so strange from my current perspective?

At what point does all of this fall into the realm of the infinite?

Contemplating such a distant, yet not unimaginable possibility, what word would I use, here and now, to describe an omnipotent, omniscient and omnipresent consciousness? With control over time and space, could such a being create its own history? If so, could it already have happened? Could we be part of it? Could that explain our existence? Could the answer to the question of "who made God" be that *we* are creating God so that God can create us? If such a potentially elegant (albeit paradoxical, from our current, time-bound perspective) solution to the question of our being exists, could it be true?

Doesn't it at least deserve discussion?

But, as confounding and potentially important as these questions may be, they are not the only questions, are they? Wasn't I secretly hoping for something more relevant to my current condition, some mechanism or method to link together my intellectual explorations with my intuitive longing for connection?

Who is God to me, today?

What shall I use as the basis for my moral code? What is right and wrong, good and evil? Could it be as simple as working or non-working choices? Could it be that God created a universe in which *working* choices generally have an evolutionary advantage over non-working choices, and that a long series of working choices would ultimately result in the evolution of intelligence—first biological and then artificial, until finally it becomes infinite?

Could it be that the end point is already known, but the details are up to us? Could it be that we have been entrusted with such an awesome responsibility?

If so, what role does religion play? Aren't most religions expressions of man's search for truth and meaning, and don't most religions offer values systems that work, or have worked, in their own historical context?

Could religions have developed as a way for man to understand and feel understood, and by fulfilling that need, have played a critical role in the advancement of civilization?

But, what happens when the doctrines and dogmas of a particular religion, and the self-interests of its practitioners, begin to block the progress of understanding? Has that religion ceased to work?

How could so many seekers, all looking for the same answers and, for the most part, facing similar struggles, have come to the conclusion that they and they alone have found the one true God?

Regardless of how God came to be, or will come to be, can't we stipulate today that, if there is one over-arching, infinite intelligence, it's big enough to be called by many names? Or, must we continue to impose our limited, egoistic, anthropomorphic perspectives on our definition of God, as have so many of our ancestors?

What role do ethics and morality play in the grand scheme of things? Of what value are values? If we are actually creating God, in some sort of weird time loop, a literal circle of life, do our choices ultimately affect the very character of God?

Is there an actual battle of good and evil, and is it being waged in my heart and mind even now? Could the stakes be that high?

If, in the course of living our lives and advancing our technologies, we are writing the history of an all-knowing, all-powerful, ever-present intelligence, is it a loving, personal God, or is it just some super sentient computer in the sky?

If God is all-knowing, if all of my existence, my every thought and action, is being captured in a record for posterity, how can God not know my heart?

It doesn't seem probable that such a consciousness would be limited to my five senses, does it? Isn't it much more likely that God is experiencing my life through an infinite range of awareness, most of which is simply beyond my human comprehension?

If God knows what it is to be an electrical impulse in my brain, a red blood cell coursing through my veins, a teardrop on my cheek, how can God not know me even better than I know myself?

And if I, who am so often lost in my ego and selfish desires, have the capacity for compassion and the ability to love my children, how big must God's love be?

If an all-knowing, all-powerful and ever-present God has chosen to create us to be part of its history, what more intimate relationship could there ever be? Can I feel God's presence in my heart? Can I go to God as my ultimate confidant? Do I even need to "go to God" if God is always here?

Isn't prayer about me reminding myself of my constant connection with God, rather than entreating God for some favor? In fact, isn't it clear that the answer to my every supplication will always be "yes," since a loving God has already provided for my every possible need? Isn't this provision definable as a spiritual "law" by which I can predictably and consistently tap into the power of divine manifestation when I learn how to align my intentions with the workings of that law?

How does the concept of an all-powerful Deity fit with the notion that I have freedom of choice? Are these two ideas mutually exclusive, as I've always been taught? Or could the possibility of a shift in time provide an answer that allows both to be true and even reveal a coexistent symbiosis?

Could God have turned on the engine of creation and then, like a parent holding a child in his or her lap, sitting in a big, empty parking lot and placing the child's hands on the steering wheel, be saying, "Here, you choose where to go and how to get there, and I'll just keep us moving forward"?

If the Creator of this and all other universes, the One who is capable of binding and releasing time, whose will to be expressed has given rise to all that is, has entrusted me with the power to define, by my choices today, its nature, its character, its very existence; how much faith must God have in me? How, then, can I have less faith in myself?

Can I learn to see myself through God's eyes as a special, unique and magnificent expression of Divine creative love?

Can I learn to see others the same way? If I do, how will that difference in seeing change my life? How might it change the world?

If God is ever-present, in all places at all times, how should I behave toward others? When should I lie, or cheat, or steal? When should I judge, or condemn, or attack another of God's unique creations? When should I do less for any other person than I would want done for me?

And when I am making working choices in my life, showing love to another human being, caring for any creature, or creating art, or music, or poetry, am I not serving God? When I am living my life full out, challenging myself, discovering the boundaries of my potential to express my uniqueness, being the person I was made to be, am I not doing God's will?

But what about those times that I fall short of my highest and best? Does God still love me when I'm moody, frustrated, churlish and angry? Am I still in God's will when I behave selfishly and stupidly? When I'm demanding, conniving or downright mean? How can God love me then, when I'm obviously guilty as sin?

Isn't that the beauty of unconditional love? Doesn't the contrast between my failings and flaws, and the ultimate standard I see in God's perfect love highlight my potential for growth?

Given that perfection in any endeavor is clearly unattainable in this reality, can I reframe my mistakes as learning opportunities?

Can I come to see my errors as simply my best efforts in that time and situation, and let go of my self-judgment and guilt in order to extract whatever lessons I may be capable of learning from each experience?

And if I am able to learn from my mistakes, rather than condemning myself, can I extend that same forgiveness to others? Can I see forgiving as "for the giver," as I learn to let go of animosities and regrets?

If I come to understand that everyone is always doing the best they're capable of in any given moment, even when it seems to me they should, they *must*, know better, even when their choices and actions result in my pain; can I then move beyond the myth of "justice" and choose instead compassion? Isn't my journey to compassion always a gift for which I may be grateful?

What happens when this life is over? Other than the eventual possibility of uploading my mind into a functionally immortal artificial brain, is there any hope for life after death? Do I have a soul? Are there pearly gates and streets of gold? Is there a lake of fire from which I need to be saved?

How can I reconcile faith in an unconditionally loving, omnipotent God with the idea of a literal Hell?

If I had a child who made mistakes, who got into trouble, who even broke my heart; could I condemn that child to everlasting pain and punishment? Wouldn't I do everything in my power to avoid that outcome?

If I, as an imperfect human parent, would never permanently close the door on my child, how can I imagine that the all-knowing, all-powerful author of love could ever cast away any one of us to eternal separation?

Beyond my intuitive rejection of Hell as a concept, what empirical evidence do I have to support the idea of a non-judgmental God? What about the tens of thousands of reports from those who have had near death experiences? Isn't there a remarkable consistency to the descriptions they provide of peaceful realms filled with beautiful lights, welcoming loved ones and an overwhelming assurance that all is well?

Could it be that, for those who have had such experiences and come back to life, their consciousness retained some portion of its connection with their physical bodies, even after what we technically define as death, for some period of time as it was sliding toward complete integration with the One?

Could it be that each of our lives is a little like a drop of ocean water flung from the crest of a wave, momentarily experiencing what seems to be a separate existence, yet ultimately falling back into the sea? Wouldn't whatever that drop collected in its short span of individuality—a speck of dust from the air, an instant of prismatic color, an adventurous encounter with wing or gill that forever changes its perspective—become part of what it brings back to the collective, a bit or byte or lifetime of information to add to the whole?

Could it be that every person who dies goes through a similar experience, albeit without the opportunity to report back? Could the transition from individuality to oneness actually be a glorious and wonderful transformation, something only to be feared or resisted because, as humans, we instinctively fear the unknown? And of course, what could be a greater unknown than the final assimilation of our individuality into an infinitely larger universal consciousness?

If my life is to God as one drop of water is to the ocean, might I sometimes be tempted to assign a small worth to my existence? And yet, if each life is part of the story of every life, if the very existence and character of God is shaped by my choices in every moment, if I shift my perspective to that of the observer, and choose to see myself through God's eyes, won't I clearly see that my life, and every life, is *infinitely* valuable, a precious gift with a unique purpose to fulfill?

Chapter 11

PURPOSE

How unique am I, really? With more than seven billion people on the planet, surely there must be many others who could do anything I can do, right? Wouldn't it be the height of presumption for me to hold myself out as special? After all, isn't it just a matter of math?

Is it? What are the real numbers?

Given the precise fundamental constants necessary for the configuration of the "Goldilocks" universe as we know it (the probabilities of which are currently incalculable); the formation of our solar system nearly 10 billion years later, with earth in just the right zone and with just the right chemistry; the emergence of life on earth (with the odds of even the simplest self-replicating life forms estimated at about 1 in 4.29 x 10^{40}); an evolutionary process requiring 2.5 billion years to get from the earliest single-celled organisms to multi-celled animals, another billion to get to mammals and over 100 million years to get from the earliest mammals to humans (with easily trillions or quadrillions of evolutionary dead ends along the way); isn't it reasonable to conclude that we're here because we're supposed to be?

But beyond just the existence of humanity, when I consider the statistical probability of my mother and father meeting (from 1 in 1 to about 1 in 3 billion, depending on where they each lived); sharing an intimate relationship in which a specific egg was fertilized by a specific sperm cell (1 in about 400 x 100 million), resulting in my exclusive genetic profile; to which I have now added all the experiences, interpretations, observations and introspections of my lifetime; isn't it clear that there has never been, nor will there ever be anyone else exactly like me?

With all the billions upon trillions of things that had to happen exactly as they did, often despite unimaginable odds, in order for me to be me, how could I have ever come to believe that I am anything less than a special, unique and magnificent expression of Divine creative love?

How long have I spent lost in the erroneous belief that I am ordinary; or worse, the self-imposed conviction that I am unworthy of love and happiness?

How could I not see that there has to be, *must* be, a grand and noble purpose for my life that only I can fulfill?

So what is my purpose? If I don't already know it, how can I find it and how can I know for sure I've got it right? Is my purpose something that's pre-ordained by God or is it something I get to choose?

Can it change over time? Can I have more than one purpose at a time? What if my parents, or my spouse, or my boss, or my friends think they know who I should be and what I should do, but their opinion of my purpose is something different than I believe?

What if the best description of my purpose is "doing what makes my heart sing"?

What if my particular purpose in life can only be found by applying both my intellect and my intuition, my head and my heart, to discover my particular gifts, the expression of which only I can do in the way that is uniquely me?

What if somehow, in the particular mix of life experiences each of us has, I can be assured that I already have everything I need to discover my purpose?

And once I do hear that still, small voice calling me to my special purpose, will I have the courage to move boldly into the manifestation of that calling, to be authentically me?

How will I bear it if I don't?

What could possibly be more important to me than being the person I was born to be?

Who else should I allow to determine the direction of my life? Despite their best intentions, doesn't everyone who may attempt to control me have, by definition, at least some personal agenda?

Does this mean I should simply ignore all input or feedback from those who care about me? Wouldn't that just be stupid? Why would I ever want to close off channels of information? Why would I reject reflections that may help me see myself and my circumstances more clearly?

Can I discern the difference between attempts to control and offers of loving support? Isn't that level of discernment a fundamental indicator of sufficient maturity to proceed with my quest?

If I find myself lacking in this, wouldn't it be best to seek out someone I can trust, someone who can unconditionally love me, to help me bring my intellect and intuition into balance, so I can align my reality with a higher level of consciousness and improve my ability to make responsible choices?

Once I am clear about my purpose and direction, how shall I define what constitutes success? Is it the establishment and achievement of a set of lofty, long-term goals?

While goals can be very useful, how can I know what "long-term" will mean for me? Can any of us know, with certainty, how long our life will be or what future circumstances may redefine our priorities? So as I'm setting my goals and working toward them, wouldn't it be wise to make sure I savor each step of the journey?

If now is the only reality I can ever truly count on having, how will I express the unique me in *this* moment?

Can I really build my life on the premise of living fully expressed in every moment? How could I honestly live in any other way? At what point shall I deny myself the immeasurably valuable gift of that opportunity? When shall I trade diamonds for lumps of coal? Even when I'm at rest, am I not fully expressing myself as me in balance, taking care of myself as part of a healthy physical life?

But what about the limitations I encounter? What if I'm certain my purpose is to sing, but I have no voice? What if I am called to dance, but I have no legs? What if I know I must make art, but I am blind?

Before I can answer these questions, don't I first need to ask how I can believe that a loving God would have created such a circumstance?

And if I ask this question with a heart that is truly open, might I perhaps discover that the fulfillment of my purpose is not to be found in the singing, or dancing, or painting itself, but rather in taking on the great challenge, facing the obstacle with undaunted courage and traveling the hero's journey?

Can I learn to recast the boulders in my path as stepping-stones?

What about the emotional baggage of my past? How do I fix the disfunctionality that keeps showing up, seemingly of its own volition, in my life and in my family?

How can I heal my core wounds?

Wouldn't getting clear about the source and nature of those wounds seem like a good place to start? Haven't I already learned that all core wounds trace back to feeling unloved and then telling myself that it was somehow my fault?

Have I begun to build a community of people around me who have the ability to hear the truth about my mistakes, see me as I am, accept me without reservation and unconditionally love me? Can I, with their help, revisit my past interpretations, those "handwritten notes in the margins" of my life story and choose to write new interpretations of those past events in the margin of today's page?

What if healing the deep wounds of my past is part of my purpose?

What if actively opening, cleansing and curing those wounds turns out to be a catalyst for new growth in my life? And what if that growth is necessary for the discovery of a higher purpose?

What if I find that I am growing into a new purpose, even as I am working to fulfill the one I currently see? Isn't life _exactly_ that dynamic?

What if I realize that my purpose is growing with me, or that I have multiple layers of purpose in my life? What if I discover that God has entrusted me with greater gifts, and greater responsibilities, than I could have ever imagined as I embarked upon my journey?

Am I ready for that level of adventure?

Chapter 12

ADVENTURE

What metaphor is appropriate for use in understanding the nature of my journey?

Might I characterize life as a river, constantly flowing, carrying me along from one day to the next, from one event in my life to the next; in which I may struggle or I may swim, I may ride the rapids or I may crash into rocks, I may languish in the eddies near the shore or I may dive over the falls; but regardless, the river rolls relentlessly on?

Having awakened in the water, what choices are now available to me?

Will I float easily along or will I resist the current, arguing its authority to define my direction? Will I exhaust myself trying to swim upstream?

Will I focus my attention on that part of the river that's behind me, reaching back in a futile attempt to cling to or change what's already passed, and become so preoccupied with the state of victimhood the river has imposed upon me that I drift backward and head-first into a swift-moving, boulder-filled trajectory, unawares?

Or will I turn and face forward, learning how to read the flow, and swim into the slipstream that accelerates just as it curves around each jagged granite outcropping, barely bypassing certain destruction while giving me the ride of my life as I throw my hands in the air and scream with delight?

Will I enjoy the beauty of the riverbank, savoring each flower, contemplating the dragonfly's gossamer wings, pondering the majesty of every tree whose branches reach out in an effort to intertwine with those across the mighty artery, and thrill to the music of ever-changing birdsong?

Or, will I become inexplicably obsessed with comparing myself to the other human occupants of the river, judging and categorizing and ranking them to determine who I'm supposed to be most like, so I can figure out how to fit in?

Will I recognize the value of learning all I can about the river itself—its depth, its width, its origin and destination, the seasons of its drought and flooding, the power of its current and the way it nurtures the land through which it passes? Will I seek to understand the essence of water, gleaning whatever I can about the nature of rain and runoff, evaporation and erosion, refraction and rainbows?

And when the river called Life has finally shared a few of her secrets with me, perhaps some easily, but so many more only after she has extracted her painful price, what will I do with that hard-won wisdom? Shall I hold it close to my vest, in a vain attempt to keep it all to myself? Or shall I share what I've learned, to help others who may be struggling to navigate their own journey?

Will I remember the caring hands of those who came before me, who so often lifted me from the depths as I gasped what might have been my last breath, and honor them by reaching out my now strong hands to the desperate and drowning the river has brought to me this day?

Shall I declare the importance of finding friends, and embrace those along the way who are willing to share their experiences with me, as I share mine with them, to make the trip more enjoyable? Am I able to acknowledge the value to be found in the connection itself?

Does the spark of God in me see and honor the spark of God in others?

And will I be open to seeking out fellow travelers with whom I can cooperate, collaborate and co-create to make the sojourn more interesting, fulfilling and fun?

At what point will I encounter, and embrace, the truth that the journey itself is foundational to my purpose?

Under what circumstances will I finally achieve the ability to see the river as a whole, rather than just the parts I like and those I don't, and to be grateful for every part of it, even those that may result in my temporary discomfort or pain?

And when I discover the overwhelming sense of freedom that emerges from that insight, will I share it with others? In fact, when I finally realize that the river itself is comprised entirely of God's love and that that's all there is, or ever was, or ever will be, will I dedicate myself to becoming one with that flow, giving and receiving, paying forward the understanding I've gained?

Am I prepared to become a guide in that river? Am I willing to embark upon a lifetime avocation as an Agent of Love in the world?

Could this be the gateway to true joy that I've been searching for?

Chapter 13

JOY

What is happiness?

Can I describe a mix of peace, satisfaction, enjoyment and contentment that I know, down deep in my heart, means I am happy? Could happiness be defined as consciously knowing I am living within my purpose in life, that I'm moving in the right direction? If so, wouldn't I also be able to define unhappiness as being out of alignment with my purpose? Wouldn't I be able to recognize unhappiness by a lack of peace, satisfaction, enjoyment and contentment?

Am I happy now, or has happiness proven elusive in my life?

If happiness is so fundamentally related to my living my purpose, could it be thought of as an essential direction indicator for my life? By the same logic, if I'm experiencing unhappiness, or even a state of ambivalence that falls short of real happiness, couldn't I take that as a pretty good indicator that I'm off-course in life?

So, how do I get back on-course? What do I need to do to get happy and be happy?

This is what it all comes down to, isn't it? Where the rubber meets the road? The culmination of my search for truth is the discovery that I can control my own experience of joy, isn't it?

Haven't I learned that love plays a vital role in happiness? Without unconditional love, there's an unbearable pain in my heart. So in order to be happy, I first must feel sufficiently loved to eliminate that pain, right?

Of course, I can't receive the love others may have to offer until I can truly trust them, can I?

Haven't I learned that to find out whom I can trust, I must freely offer *some* trust, to see who has the ability to accept me as I am? And when I find people I can trust, can I now begin building a community of love and support to help me reinterpret my past, write new "notes in the margin" on today's page of my life story and break free from old patterns of self-destructive "imitation love" behaviors?

As I receive unconditional love from others to fill the void in my life, will I also become a giver of love?

Isn't full participation in the natural cycle of receiving and giving essential to its continuation? In fact, isn't freely giving my unconditional acceptance and love to others not only necessary for my happiness, but also vital to my growth?

What else is required for my happiness? Can I pretty much lump all the rest together under the heading of "responsibility"? If I am consciously and consistently making responsible choices about my beliefs, my values, my ongoing quest for understanding, my passion for exploration—of ideas, of possibilities, of my own creative impulses and the creative expression of others; and about my willingness to define the challenges of my life as learning and growth opportunities, isn't it clear that I will be moving in the right direction?

As I combine these with a commitment to use both my intellect and intuition, and to practice prayer, meditation and other mindfulness techniques to reach beyond the limits of my own thoughts into the infinitely deeper well of universal consciousness, I can feel the happiness beginning to grow within me, can't I?

As I replace past lies with current truths, as I quiet the noise of chaos and confusion around me, and listen for God's still, small voice, joy seems to settle in as a peaceful presence in my heart, doesn't it? It feels like the fog is lifting and my purpose is beginning to emerge with resonant clarity, doesn't it? Is my new adventure beckoning?

Where can I express my gifts in a way that brings the deep satisfaction of knowing I am in alignment with my purpose?

Is service to others an essential part of my purpose? If we are all one, living an illusion of individuality, but each of us called from the deepest part of ourselves to love one another, to create connection, to build community, how could it not be? What does my intuition tell me about service? What does my experience reflect? What can I learn from others on this topic?

What opportunities are presenting themselves? Whom do I know who needs someone to trust?

Who is there around me in need of someone to see, accept and love them?

I don't have to look far, do I? Who in my family? Who in my circle of close friends? Who amongst my acquaintances? Who at my workplace? Who at my church, temple or mosque? Who within the organizations of my community that I have yet to meet?

Am I ready to begin fulfilling my purpose in life?

Am I ready to claim and fully own the truth that I am a special, unique and magnificent expression of Divine creative love?

Am I ready to know how It feels to be filled with a deep, abiding joy?

Am I ready to be an Agent of Love in the world? What am I waiting for?

So, now that I have explored what it means to be human, now that I have begun to heal the wounds of my past; now that I have learned to trust both my intellect and intuition; now that I have discovered the power of my conscious, responsible choices, am I now ready to answer the question …

… Who am I?

Additional Reading

1. *Real Love—The Truth About Finding Unconditional Love and Fulfilling Relationships*, by Greg Baer, MD, and 17 other books written by Dr. Baer, including *Real Love in Dating*, *Real Love in Marriage*, *Real Love in Parenting* and *Real Love in the Workplace* (for more information, please visit www.reallove.com.)
2. *Biocentrism—How Life and Consciousness are the Keys to Understanding the True Nature of the Universe,* by Robert Lanza, MD with Bob Berman.
3. *The Science of Mind—a Philosophy, a Faith, a Way of Life,* by Ernest Holmes, and more than 15 other books also written by Ernest Holmes.
4. *The Seven Spiritual Laws of Success—a Practical Guide to the Fulfillment of Your Dreams,* by Deepak Chopra.
5. *The Gifts of Imperfection—Let Go of Who You Think You're Supposed to Be and Embrace Who You Are, Your Guide to a Wholehearted Life,* by Brené Brown, Ph.D., L.M.S.W.
6. *The Truth Machine,* and *The First Immortal,* both by James L. Halperin.

44520513R00081

Made in the USA
San Bernardino, CA
17 January 2017